Susan Rose lost everything in 1989 when she became psychotic with a life threatening disorder. Her house, kids, job, marriage and health all disintegrated. It was impossible keeping her highs and lows in check. It was like walking on an invisible tightrope, waiting for the dreadful fall. She worked hard to break through a reality beyond time. This is the story of how Rose wiggled through a hole in the universe and regained her sanity.

Madness Broke The Rose walks the reader through Susan's fight with bipolar disorder and takes them on a journey through time as Susan recollects her reality during her life's struggles to Hell and back. She finds humor in even the most serious moments and ultimately forgives herself for the affliction of pain on herself and others. In turn, there is a healing from the painful memories of the past. Susan leaves the reader with no escape and tells the truth, the raw truth, even through the most embarrassing moments, leaving nothing to the imagination.

Madness
Broke
The Rose

Susan Rose

Photo of the author in 1989, prior to her freefall into madness

To Jhena Faeran, my editor: Your talent as an author, poet and musician has made not only poetry and music from my words; you, dear friend, have created a symphony of my book, Madness Broke the Rose. Thank you. There are no words that describe what you have done with my story

Sincerely,

Susan

To Susan Rose, author of Madness Broke the Rose, during this project I was frequently struck by your exuberance and elegant word choice. It has been an honor to capture your unique voice.

Sincerely,

Jhena

TABLE OF CONTENTS

Writing my life story was a chilling pursuit of details
about my life experiences.
I had to learn what actually transpired.
My mind was a raging inferno
that abruptly sank into the quagmire,
misery beyond human understanding.
I journeyed to accept a long and treacherous road
with a crippling mental illness, bipolar one disorder;
this demon attempted to swallow me whole.
This demon ensured a path
of numerous life-threatening suicides.
But I triumphed over this adversity.
Bond with me;
side by side travel with me
on the journey through
"*insanity...*"
always knowing our mundane reality
waits for us on the other side.

My head is in a paper bag; I can't get out! Pain floods my inner being and I have no peace. There is no escape from this unbearable torture. My mind is a runaway train with no brakes. When I manage some sleep in snatches, my soul descends into a black bottomless pit. Numbers and words form and disappear at an alarming rate. My body turns numb as my thoughts vanish into thin air. Time stands still and everyone is a statue except me. Other people are unaware that my mind, spirit and body dance in different realities at the same time. Sex becomes the driving force in my life—sex without limits. To seduce or be seduced is the primary objective.

This was my dream state that lasted six years, when time stopped. I danced with the devil in my depression; I danced with the Angels and was euphoric when I became one with the universe.

This was my freefall into insanity.

INNOCENCE LOST

I was violated by a doctor of my youth;
my purity and innocence fled...
my first introduction to sexuality,
festers like an open wound inside me,
unable to heal.
I was only four years old
when the vicious events started.
I couldn't run;
I couldn't hide;
my legs were cut off at the knees
and my arms glued to my back.
I was unable to push him away.
That monster managed to die in his sleep.
Could he ask for a better exit?

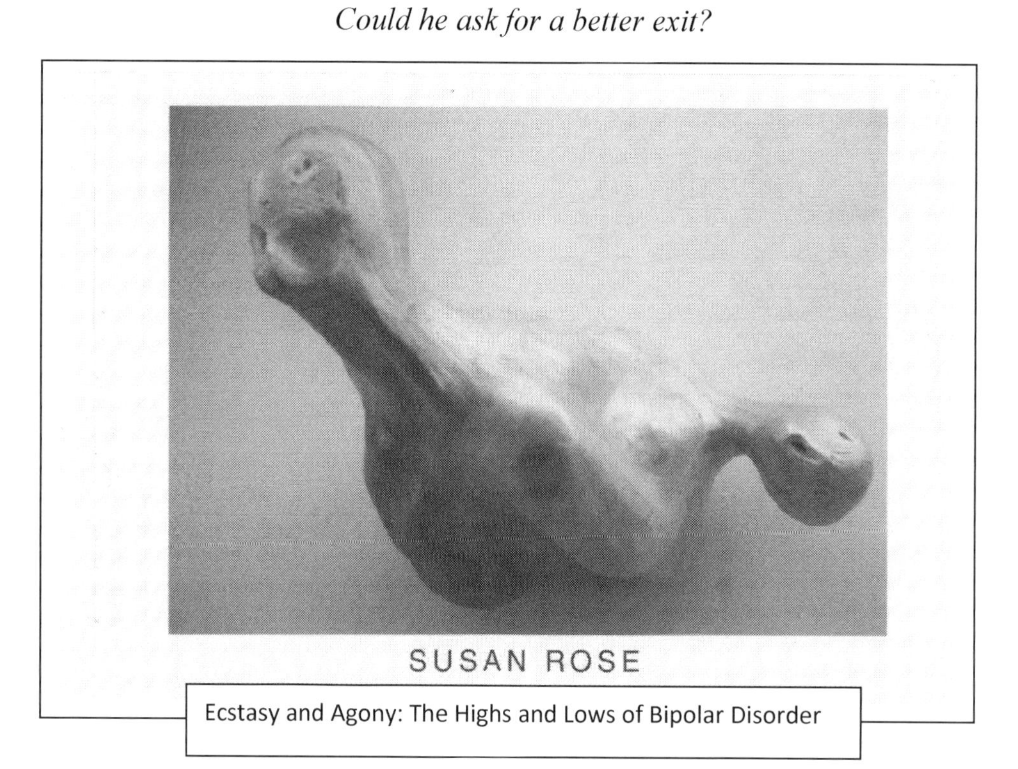

Ecstasy and Agony: The Highs and Lows of Bipolar Disorder

"The farther backward you can look,
the farther forward you can see."
- Winston Churchill

When I think back, I go to the very first time I was violated, by a doctor in my youth and my purity and innocence fled. This, my first introduction to sexuality, festers like an open wound inside me, unable to heal. The sadness stays with me and I never completely resolved it.

When I was a child, I outlined all the pictures in my coloring book, then colored within the lines. This was the way I told the world my boundaries were being violated. There was no other way to express what was happening. Even if I could, I don't think anyone would have believed me. Doctors were put on a pedestal as if they were gods. I would be labeled a liar.

The doctor never touched my sister Doris. When I told my mother what had gone on, she was in denial and said, "I was always with you during your office visits with him."

However, she wasn't there when Dad took me; he left me alone with the doctor. It wasn't his fault. How could he have known what went on behind that closed door?

I was only four years old when the vicious events started. I was always dressed in a johnny. When the doctor examined me, he always removed it. Something seemed wrong about this. It felt odd, but there was no way to stop it. He would tell me to bend over and touch my toes.

I clearly remember him with a needle and syringe walking toward me as I lie on the examining table, always nude. His snow white hair is the one memory that is fixed, running through my mind like a movie, repeating itself over and over again.

Once he took my nipples in his fingers and said slyly, "Don't these work well!" I felt something hard against my leg during examinations and it wasn't his stethoscope. I was too young to know what it was then but now I am convinced it was his erection.

I was wide awake and very alert at that moment. I felt ashamed and grabbed the johnnie from his hand to cover my body. I am not sure what age I was. I do remember he was at the foot of the examining table at this moment. That is the last thing I recall.

I don't think my parents would have believed me if I told them what was happening. I felt helpless and so, so alone. I couldn't stop this abuse. I couldn't run; I couldn't hide; my legs were cut off at the knees and my arms glued to my back. I was unable to push him away.

Every visit he gave me antibiotics that he said were penicillin, but I wasn't a sickly child. There was no reason for it. I always wondered why, but as a minor I didn't question it. He said it was penicillin, but who knows if it was really penicillin or a means of blocking my memory? Paranoia strikes, but there is some truth to paranoia.

I wanted to draw, so Grandma bought me an art set. There was a book with instructions, pencils and paper. I remember trying to draw peoples' faces. As I recall I did a good job, but the faces were the only thing I drew and then I put the pencil away. I had no motivation or encouragement from home or school and the art classes weren't like the ones today.

I drew the lines as messages, my way to tell the world what was happening. My borders were desecrated on a regular basis, but I could draw within the lines, the only way I knew to save myself. But no one got the meaning. These lines became my fortress, but it wasn't strong enough to keep that doctor away. My invisible walls weren't high enough; I was just a little baby. Why did he do this?

As I write this, negative emotions seize my chest and I have a feeling of choking. Even today, this man haunts me in my dreams. He died in his sleep! Does he know he died because I nearly had the full picture of what was happening all those years?

Something bizarre occurred when I got to this chapter. Black and blue marks, as if caused by fingers, appeared on my right arm. Was I getting too close to what had happened to me? Could he be trying to pull me in?

I never prayed, but when I was a child mother said a reassuring prayer before I went to sleep: *Now I lay me down to sleep, I pray the lord my soul to keep and if I should die before I wake, I pray the Lord my soul to take.* I said this prayer for months and the marks disappeared.

The doctor had a photo of his wife and five daughters hanging on his office wall. My memory of the photo stands out so clearly even today. Who would think a doctor with a loving family could be a child molester, a monster? When I think of the five young daughters in the image, I wonder if they were fatalities.

Reflecting on all that happened in my childhood world is an intrusion to my psyche. That monster managed to die in his sleep. Could he ask for a better exit? Where is the justice? He died before I could be his accuser. Can I forgive him? Was that his nature? Was that how and what he was?

An enormous amount of Catholic priests have been accused and sentenced for acting out on their desires and molesting children. These children, did they forgive? Should I forgive? I would say in a shaky voice, “I will forgive. I won't forget. I will carry the hidden memories to my grave.” These memories are pushed so deep, god help me if they surface.

On my last visit the doctor said, “I know of a prostitution ring. Would you be interested in participating?”

I was 17 years old at the time. I said nothing and thought to myself, *Did I really hear that?* Today I can say I sure did! What happened all those years? Something must have happened, something I can't remember. A prostitution ring, what was that all about? Why would I be interested in such things? I can't put the pieces of the puzzle together. Maybe it's better this way.

In those days there were no laws keeping nurses in the room to protect the patient and doctor. Now there are laws that a doctor cannot examine a patient without a nurse present, to prevent such behavior or accusations of said behavior. This was one of the greatest laws ever established.

The doctor’s office had an overwhelming medicinal smell in the air. As an adult the scent of alcohol brought back memories of his abuse. In hospital settings, there is no avoiding the smell of alcohol. It was used for everything when I worked in them. I wondered why I liked the smell. You might think I would hate it.

I discussed this with a fellow employee, who said smells trigger memories, memories which pour through the senses. Suddenly things were clearer in my past recollections, but only a few; for years I dismissed them. The smell evokes feelings today with its same profound fragrance. I remember the medicinal odors of the doctor’s office of my youth, the strong smell of alcohol. It permeates my nostrils, branding scars into thin membranes.

Bright overhead lights are a trigger for me. They make me feel uneasy, make my head spin. When I was about nineteen, I had surgery for a benign tumor in my left breast. I no longer visited the doctor of my youth and yet he was looking down at me. I saw him as clear as day, his snow white hair shining through the overhead lights as he said to the anesthesiologist, “Isn’t Susan beautiful?”

Then everything went dark and feelings of no control took over, the same as the feelings of the child in that doctor's grip, the same feeling I had when being molested by him. There was no reason for him to be in that room and yet there he was. What goes through my mind right now is *What did they do to me?*

At one point I worked in a tiny claustrophobic office with a fluorescent light directly over my head. I wanted a lamp in the office instead of that fluorescent light like the operating room, but everyone was against it. I appealed to the boss for the lamp; he saw no problem and agreed.

However, my associates disregarded my feelings and took the lamp away. I was hurt but I gave in and accepted it. If they knew the real reason, the lamp would have remained, though even I didn't know why it affected me so negatively.

In 2001, I read an article about an anesthesiologist who was arrested. He was having oral sex with the patients he put under for surgery. This was devastating news to me as I recalled the doctor of my youth being in the operating room during my surgery, back in the 1950s when rules weren't so stringent. It made me question once again why he was there and what he could get away with while I was under the anesthesia.

I tried not to be paranoid, but how could I not; I was still blameless then. I had no knowledge of my mental illness and the enormous part it played in my mother's family. My mother passed the gene of mental illness down to me. All these devastating emotional blows were placed deep within my mind, keeping my mental illness dormant until middle age.

If there was anything good about these traumatic experiences, it was that madness did not hit until I was 37 years old.

Much later in life I found an article in the local newspaper about a pediatrician in Maryland who molested sixteen patients. He used video cameras to record some of the brutal attacks. Disney themes such as Pinocchio decorated his wall.

The investigating detective, who had viewed thousands of molestation images, said these were some of the most disturbing that he ever saw. The article touched home with me. The doctor was 56 years old, about the same age as the doctor that assaulted me.

I remember a reoccurring nightmare of snakes wrapping themselves around my legs, causing severe pain. Mom would end the aches by rubbing my legs. I don't remember when the nightmares stopped, but the doctor said, "It's just growing pains."

Growing pains my ass! He'd been a wicked monster through this period and beyond. I want to scream right now!

In the Freudian perspective, a snake or serpent is a phallic symbol. No wonder I was dreaming of snakes squeezing my legs and having the pain. I want to shriek, pull out my hair, bang my head against the wall from the memories.

You white-haired bastard! You're already dead; stabbing you in the heart isn't good enough! Shredding you into pieces is more like it!

These feelings are past anger, fury, rage, suffering for eternity. None of these words can describe my sorrow and the pain in my abdomen as I speak about these moments.

The second, third and fourth grades are a blur. The only things I remember during this time period were doctor visits and house calls. I can see his snow white hair clearly in my mind. I can hear him say to mom, "Isn't Susan beautiful!"

As I write these words the anger building is visible.

This was the basic foundation, the commencement of numerous molestations; yes, my family doctor, thief of innocence. Right now I feel it *(RAGE! I SEE RED! MY BRAIN IS ON FIRE!)* There is no name hideous enough to describe his actions.

My recollections are pasted to my brain. I want to know the whole story, so the puzzle pieces fit together to make me whole. I am still half a person because of it; there are countless mysteries that haven't been explored.

Much later in life I did a painting called *Screeches: Self-Harm.* The medium was charcoal and red lipstick. It was a portrait of me at ten years old, in a very submissive pose, without legs and my arms behind my back.

Taking a board with protruding nails, I scratched the portrait, leaving the appearance of subtle lines. I never ever scratched myself. I can identify with self-afflicted injury, the concealed subconscious slightly revealing itself. Grooves covering the self-portrait became the cover of the book.

As with the doctor of my youth, I couldn't escape: legs incomplete, no feet, incapable of running, of hiding… hiding where? Innocent, blameless, tiny me, powerless. No defenses, imprisoned as his captive.

"You won't find safety here; it's in another universe far, far away."

CHILDHOOD: PIECES OF PETALS, PIECES OF THORNS

We had a strange family. My grandpa was half American-Indian and an alcoholic. The gene of madness may have started with him. My great-grandmother was a full-blooded American Indian.

Grandmother was proud of her heritage. I think that's where my straight, shiny, jet black hair is from

This was all I knew of my history. But mental illnesses, too numerous to write about, were prevalent in the entire family tree. I didn't have full information about the tornado-like effect mental illness would play in my future.

Our family lived in my grandparents' house until I was four. Then we moved to a third floor apartment. Just below was a canal to the roaring Blackstone River. Mom, my sister Doris and I walked the canal many times. The Blackstone River was appropriately named; it was pitch black.

Grandmother Lora lived close by. My grandparents' household became my safe place. No one could touch me there. When I stepped over the threshold, peace of mind followed; even thinking about it helped me. It was a short bicycle ride over the bridge. I would go to gram's every day I could.

On special occasions my grandmother Lora bought my sister and I dolls. Girls played with dolls. I was a tomboy and played with the boys. I played touch football, baseball and horseshoes. Dolls had no place in my life. My masculine side was more developed and stronger than my feminine side.

In mom's family there were seven sisters and two brothers. The seven sisters owned only one nice dress and had to share when going out on a Saturday night.

My mother's sisters Amy, Nancy and Gloria were definitely strange. The women ran naked through the streets. They did so many outlandish acts. It was very embarrassing to those around them.

There were no medications in those days or understanding of mental illness. People with mental illness were generally put into insane asylums for life.

Later the three sisters were institutionalized and remained there for life because of their bizarre behavior. I don't know much about them.

My parents were blue-collar workers. They never went out to eat, but they took my sister and me to lots of the movies downtown. One time I saw a boy standing in line at the refreshment counter buying popcorn. He had the latest hairstyle of the times; his hair formed a banana curl that dangled in the center of his brow. I was about ten-years-old and really thought he was the cat's meow. *("Isn't he gorgeous!")*

Mother favored my sister Doris. They had the same personality, while my father and I shared the same personality. We were the peacemakers. My mother and sister were more aggressive. My father always agreed with my mother so they never fought.

We were poor, but there was never drug or alcohol abuse. The only abuser was my mother and it was directed towards my brother and I; we were always feeling her wrath. Mother loved me, but it took a long time to show it. She was about sixty-five before we had a decent relationship. Mom never expressed love. Dad showed it sometimes, but only said it once: "I love you."

To this day I wonder, "Did I hear that?"

Happy-go-lucky: this was the nickname my mother gave me as a child. How bizarre. Looking at my pictures as a child, I see a maniacal grin, with teeth clenched the same way I clench them now when manic.

My main lesson in kindergarten was abuse toward me. The teacher grabbed the pencil in my hand and threw it.

"It's too small!" she screamed hysterically. She embarrassed, shamed and humiliated me. "Your picture's ugly and you don't know right from left!"

I remember clearly a piece of white paper in front of me on my desk. There were two hands drawn. One hand had a big R on it and the other a big L but even with this I was still confused.

"Stupid, your class picture is ugly."

This so-called teacher secured my fate. Ugly, stupid, stammer, failure…

Having a speech impediment made words hard to pronounce. Mom and my teachers in grade school called me stupid and it stuck with me countless years. I received poor grades and stayed back a year. The thoughts in my head were going too fast, due to my mental illness at this early age. I was unable to read, spell, write, or concentrate. Basically, I was a mess. When I had to read out loud I would read one sentence, cry and then sit down.

"Stupid!"

There were no funds for transportation so Doris and I walked and hiked embankments and endured the elements in order to reach school. As far back as I can remember there were no school cancellations due to bad weather.

Doris used to read to me all the time; no wonder I couldn't concentrate while reading. I had Attention Deficit Disorder and mental illness going on as far back as I can remember.

"Doris, stop reading to Susan, let her read on her own," said mom.

Sister didn't listen to mom and read me the comic strips in the Sunday pepper. Doris's favorite comic was "Nancy."

I never read a full book until I was 28—Salem's Lot by Steven King, about vampires. When I finished the book I was fascinated by them.

Daydreaming was frequent. My make-believe dream-fantasy world evolved; it was a key symptom of delusions at this early age.

Playing outside and racing by an open window, a snake lunged at me. Mom dismissed this also. Dancing with fairies, elves and imps, I would skip, hop and bounce from one stepping-stone to another, leaving at sunset. This became my preferred play time. Mother discouraged and discounted my involvement with these tiny creatures.

I used to put fire flies in a jar and it was as if I was catching fairies; that was a happier time, not like the yellow and black spiders.

Night terrors began at age five with Dracula biting my neck. I felt his fangs puncture my skin. This experience disappeared when I changed position but it was too hard. I felt trapped, then the pressure on my neck gradually showed its presence; this was the beginning of night terrors.

My sister Doris's bed was my safest place even though she wet the bed. I didn't care, that's how terrified I was. Darkness and shadows from the window frightened me. Could they be shadow people?

These night terrors persisted even as an adult; today they are gone.

Lifting my skirt and showing my slip was my first seductive action. I had an intensified sexual awakening at the early age of six. Innocence no longer existed. This mental illness was present, triggering these feelings.

One day the old woman next door asked, "I have a floor that needs washing. Who would like the job?"

I said, "I would!"

I told my mother, "Mother, Betty needs her floor washed."

Mom said, "Is she going to pay you?"

I said, "Yes, fifty cents."

Mom said, "Make sure you do a good job." The floor was black and white. I scrubbed it clean. She was happy with the results. This was my first paycheck and now I was worth something.

Summer days were hot, hazy and humid, with temperatures so high they were suffocating. I could barely breathe. Enormous quantities of clammy sweat turned my bed into a swimming pool.

My bedroom was so small, it resembled a burial chamber. It was so severely claustrophobic it was like an airtight casket. The room was gloomy and dark and shadows from the window scared me. When there was a lightning storm I gazed out the window. It was fascinating to me.

The barber strap was used as punishment. "If you duck again, I'll hit you," Mother shouted. She hit me so much, I ducked when she crossed my path. Why did mom call me happy-go-lucky? If this was an indication of my personality, why all the beatings? The barber strap was used on her as a child. Was this learned behavior or was it more than that?

My mother hit me and my brother but never touched my sister, maybe because she didn't have a mental illness. There was something about me and my brother that my mother didn't like.

Could we have been acting out because of our mental illness and Mother saw herself in us? I can't be completely positive. My sister and mother were easy to anger, whereas my dad and I were the peacemakers. My brother didn't favor either mom or dad.

It took a lifetime for Doris and me to communicate with each other. With my mania I was unable to listen to her. I was the one who was constantly talking.

When I became stable she said, "You can listen!"

She was tickled pink. All my life she acted as though she was my mother and treated my brother the same way. I don't think she knew what she was doing, but had good intentions.

My sister was openly jealous of me most of my life. She said, "Men age eight to eighty like you. What is it you have that they like so much?" I think they noticed my manic personality.

Mother divorced my father during a manic episode. She was always rational except for this one time. She started acting like she was fifteen years old. It could have been in response to her change of life. She was never diagnosed with Bipolar Disorder and never hospitalized. When she complained about her nerves, her doctor gave her Valium for short periods.

Mom died of lung cancer at age 77. She was on a hospice regime. But things didn't work out very well.

My sister would visit her every day, bring her favorite cookies and try to comfort her.

I was a three hour drive away and didn't spend as much time with her as my sister did.

She loved my mother so deeply. I wasn't there at her bedside when she passed away. No one should have to die alone. I don't remember, but my sister and her husband Ron must've been there.

Dad never yelled or hit me. I have so many fond loving moments with dad. We spent many hours at a sand bank placing old bottles and cans to shoot with dad's 22-caliber rifle and shot gun.

I begged him to let me shoot the shot gun.

"It will knock you on your ass," he slyly said and it did; my shoulder hurt for weeks.

My father "Mack" only reached sixth grade. He was a product of the Second World War. He witnessed much bloodshed during his four year stay in the navy. He fought on the beaches of Normandy and the deserts of Africa, where he had the opportunity to see General Patton. He saw the famous ivory pistol grip handle in Patton's holster.

Patton made sure everyone knew they were ivory, saying, "Only a pimp from a cheap New Orleans whorehouse would carry a pearl-handled pistol."

Dad and I made up nicknames for each other. Dad called me "Big ears" and I called him "crazy horse.

Dad was no saint. He slept with Mom's sister Amy; she got pregnant and had a boy. The baby was born in New York City. No one knows if he was adopted. No one ever talked about him and no one knows what truly happened to him. I asked Dad if this was true. I had a brother who was also a cousin that I never knew about. How bizarre is that?

Dad remarked, "Yes, when I was young I never thought about consequences."

I was forty when he told me. I wanted to find the boy, but my sister was dead set against it.

Today I think about my brother/cousin. I believe he was named Joseph after his grandfather Joe on my mother's side of the family. I wonder if he had a happy life. I also wonder if he had to suffer the consequences of the family's history with mental illness. He would have had no knowledge of anything in his bloodline.

When dad and I walked in the woods and on the railroad tracks, he would say, "Susan, listen to the birds talk." Dad died when he was 77 and now when the chickadee sings I say "Hi, Dad." I miss those days.

There was a science fair every year in grammar school. My project was about the brain. I didn't need an abnormal brain like the Frankenstein monster; a cow would do just fine.
Dad took me to the slaughterhouse. A cow hung upside down from its heels. They put a bucket underneath her throat and sliced it with a knife. Then a large moo sounded; the tongue dangled in the air and dripping blood filled the pan. They sliced her abdomen and out came a small calf. Of course it was dead.

Within minutes I had a warm brain in the palm of my hands, to be placed in a jar with fluid for the science fair.

Dad stayed outside. He said, "I saw too much bloodshed in the war. I can't watch. But Susan, you should become a doctor, nothing seems to bother you."

Yes, I was intelligent. The truth is if my mental illness were caught when I was young anything might have been possible. I could've been the butcher, the baker, the candlestick maker! A brain surgeon… maybe a radiologist, that's the real dream job!

Mom came with me to the science fair. She looked so pretty, all dressed up, with lipstick on and wearing a fine hat. I never saw mom look so beautiful.

As we entered the parking lot kids were yelling, "Susan, you won first prize."

I wanted to cry. I knew it was impossible for me to win first prize. The kids were just being mean to me again.

My project was at the back of the auditorium. It was hard to find, but as I drew closer I saw the ribbon. It was true!

I only saw my dad get angry at my mother once. He wanted some tires out of the cellar. My mother said they were going to stay in the cellar. My dad told her, "I'm bringing the tires up and that's that." He stuck to his guns. Mom backed off and that was the end of it. This was a big argument for my parents and the only argument that dad won.

My father never had friends. He said, "People equal problems."

I'd sit outside on the front step. When Dad came out I'd ask, "Where are you going, Dad?"

He took me everywhere he went. Sometimes we would go to the drugstore. I'd get vanilla soda and buy Superman comic books and baseball cards. When I was with my father he would strike up a conversation with a perfect stranger for hours.

We also went to Narragansett Airport. Every year "The Blue Angels" jets flew close in formation like geese. We went to see them every year for five years until two planes collided in an unfortunate accident that we didn't witness. After that the show stopped.

My dad always taught me to be responsible for myself. He often said, "Get off one bus and another one comes along," meaning that when one relationship ends another takes its place. That is what my dad used to tell me.

He also said, "Be nice to the people on the way up because you might meet them on the way down." "One day you will look in the mirror and see an old woman… but you will feel the same inside."

Dad never helped me. This was a stepping stone to maturity at a young age. When I was forty I lived with dad for two years because I lost my car and job, sick with my mental illness. It was so different living with him as an adult than it was from a child's eyes. He hadn't changed, he was just older.

Even at the end of his life, when he died he left me nothing except memories, but they were all good. His new wife, Sandy, got all of his money and possessions. When I was visiting him in his hospital room, she would enter. Sandy never left me alone with my father. She was afraid he might change his will and give his children the house.

Dad died at home. When I went to visit him, Sandy wouldn't let me in his room, though he was close to death and on oxygen. I could only get a glimpse of him. This made me extremely angry. Sandy made it so I was unable to say goodbye to my dying dad.

But there was one thing his wife couldn't take from me and that was the love between a father and his daughter. That was mine.

I make it my job to leave some history for my kids. During vacations I pick them up something special. Pieces of art, photos and other items became my history, with stories that go along with them.

MR. RIGHT WAS MR. WRONG

LUKE

My mind was on off and I never asked questions.

I married Luke because he asked me. I followed his wants and needs. I had no voice. He was the puppeteer and I was the puppet. I hate telling this story because I feel like a fool.

Our sex life was nothing to brag about; this was the "Slam Bam Thank You Ma'am" era. At times I was unreceptive to his affections. In one instance he pinned me to the wall and as you might say, did his business. This was a fine line, forcing me like this; how was I to stop him?

We were about to go to dinner with his mom; I wore a beautiful white dress. He wanted sex before we left; in a nasty voice he said, "I want it now. We have time."

I said, "No."

That was the wrong word. He pushed me down and forced me to have sex. Back then I didn't consider it rape. I thought he had the right, as if I were bought and paid for, but now I see it was rape.

This incident played a big part in becoming subservient to men. I always seemed to be in the wrong place at the wrong time. As nightfall's shadows appeared, one after another, year after year, my very soul was overshadowed and trapped in the torture chamber I called "Me."

I was married at sixteen years of age; my husband was eighteen. We wanted a church wedding and had a conference with a priest but he said, "You're too young."

He refused to marry us. We had no choice so we were married at City Hall in Pawtucket, Rhode Island. I wore a white dress with white shoes. He wore a coat and tie. Only the immediate family attended.

My family had no choice but to accept the marriage. It wasn't a shotgun marriage; I was not pregnant. "Stupid" was tattooed to my forehead for almost the rest of my life.

Luke and I lived in a second floor apartment with little light. The hallway was pitch-black. I was afraid of the dark. I would run up the stairs as fast as I could. I always felt like there was someone behind me, but who or what? I was just a child, sixteen years old and pregnant. I wanted to scream, cry and yell, "Help!" But there was none.

We had a son who we named Eugene. When I went into the hospital to have the baby, the nurses standing outside my door said, "She's a baby having a baby."

I didn't know they were talking about me, but they were and they were absolutely right.

Luke drank Jack Daniels whiskey and was a mean drunk. He threw things and poured coffee over my head.

He slyly said, "Hit Susan on the head and she will come up laughing."

Yet I never fought back. He was six foot two inches and weighed one hundred eighty pounds.

Every Saturday night, Luke and I went dancing at The Playboy Bunny Club. The lights were dim and the waitresses wore playboy bunny costumes complete with white tails and black fishnet stockings. The line went into the street; that's how popular the place was.

I loved to dance; it was an escape from reality for me.

After our divorce, Luke remarried almost right away and had three children, two girls and one boy. He said, "Susan, when you can't dance anymore, no man will want you."

If he were still alive I would happily say, "I'm 65 and I dance like I'm 24." (In the morning I feel like I'm 92, but it's worth it.) Dancing has always been a world only I could enter, my safe place. Dancing was my coping mechanism and I didn't even know it; dancing, sun, other exercises…instead of the familiar emotional shut down.

Because of abuse, memories were too horrifying to face. My mind would crack like Humpty Dumpty. All the king's horses and all the king's men couldn't put

Humpty Dumpty back together again. If you cracked this egg open, this would be my fate; tougher again, this crackpot… I mean cracked egg.

Luke's father was an alcoholic who never missed a day of work. He was also a chain smoker, with fingertips stained a yellowish brown color. His son's fingers were the same. Both died at fifty from complications related to smoking and drinking.

Although Luke was a very intelligent man, he couldn't keep a job for long. He decided to go to college. He majored in accounting at Johnson and Wales College in Providence, Rhode Island. I did not finish high school, in part because I felt I wasn't good enough. But the main reason was I was about to marry. Married people don't attend high school so I forfeited my high school years, leaving in the ninth grade. There would be no senior prom for me.

I remember walking downstairs that day, crying all the way down. There were quite a few steps and a whole lot of tears. My mother wanted to stop the marriage and send me to my aunts in Canada but dad said, "Let her do what she wants."

Later in life dad explained his decision in a solemn voice. "Susan, one of your mother's relatives has to be locked in her room at night, violent and irrational to herself and others. I know this for a fact, Susan and who knows what else would await you. This would not be a healthy environment for you and there may be other things we just don't know about. All three of your mother's sisters are in asylums."

I think dad's decision was right. It was better to marry young than to live in insanity and chaos in Canada.

Luke started to cheat on me early on, when I was nineteen. That was the final blow that made me make the decision to go. I was still able to make decisions. My mental illness didn't get in the way yet and this marriage had to end. This time period marked the beginning of multiple rapes in my life.

ISAAC

Because I survived many forms of abuse as a child, I had created a wall that could not be penetrated. I felt safe behind that wall. I could not feel, but I also could not be reached. Behind that wall, I said to the world, "You cannot break me."

However, I was broken by my second husband, Isaac. He needed to control me and so he broke down my wall. Whatever he wanted from me he received. He used a wrecking ball of criticism and in my need for approval, I was defenseless. Defeated, I became his prisoner and something inside of me gave up.

When I was Assistant Chief in the respiratory department, Isaac began work in my department. The first time I saw Isaac a black ribbon was pinned on the lapel of his shirt, indicating bereavement. His sister Nancy, just fourteen, had died.

When Isaac was sitting at his desk writing notes about a patient, I leaned forward and pressed my body against his back. Heat radiated from my skin; he commented on my warmth.

Isaac had just returned from the Vietnam War, where he served as a medic. It was Isaac's experience with first aid and emergency medicine in Vietnam that helped him land his first job.

He told me how once during a firefight, he was in a fox hole when a mortar shell hit his medic bag. Although he suffered perforated eardrums and hemorrhages in his lungs, the medic bag took all the shrapnel, ultimately saving his life.

Isaac was the only man in that platoon who was not killed that night. His injuries saved his life; they med evacuated him out of that god forsaken place back to the USA. His wounds took him to Walter Reed Naval hospital in California, where he had many operations on his perforated ear drums. Although Isaac regained full hearing in one ear it took nine months to repair the damage and he still had minimal hearing in his other ear.

To this day I can't remember whether the severe hearing loss was in Isaac's right or left ear, but he always got upset with me when I talked into his damaged ear. I couldn't help it. I can't tell my own right from left most of the time. But Isaac thought that I didn't care enough about him to pay attention to his problem.

I thought that being Jewish, Isaac would make a good father, husband and provider. I made the biggest mistake of my life. I married for all the wrong reasons: money, prestige, Isaac's loving family and a father for my son. I didn't love him, but although it wasn't the best marriage, I learned to love him a little. And he did have some good qualities… but not enough.

Isaac introduced me to his mom and dad, both caring individuals. They conveyed their fondness for me in many ways. I wanted to be a part of this close-knit Jewish family. They welcomed me because I converted to Judaism. His mother passed away before the divorce.

What I remember most about our wedding was smashing the wine glass at the end of the ceremony. Both sides of the family were at the wedding; religious beliefs didn't stand in the way of a happy moment.

My underlying mental illness didn't help any. I felt ugly, stupid and worthless and Isaac made sure it stayed this way. I was more than a great mother and wife, always agreeing to his every wish; I was a slave!

I had no time for myself and never used a baby sitter. Socializing with other women was impossible. My one and only friend was Jude.

Isaac didn't like her. He actually brought a woman home to be my "friend" but this did not work out. How could it? Even I saw through it. When Isaac didn't have control over me, he was out of control. He was sometimes physically abusive, but his emotional abuse was worse.

One time we were driving home and with no warning Isaac punched me across the bridge of my nose. This happened right out of the blue; there was no rhyme or reason for this act of aggression. My nose was swelling and I was in pain so I went to Emerson Hospital. The blow had cracked the cartilage but not the bone. I'd had enough and told Isaac I would leave him if he didn't stop hitting me.

He stopped but the emotional abuse continued. I would have stayed with Isaac if my mental illness hadn't played a huge part in ending the marriage. I was flying high, out of control, like a jet plane in a downward spin that at any moment could smash into pieces, just another metaphor for madness.

For me emotional pain is worse than physical. Gaining self-esteem was firmly forbidden; Isaac always had his way. There was no escape but the dike was about to burst. The immense force of the water behind it drowned the bastard.

Being openly abusive was part of Isaac's control issue. When I gained self-confidence he bashed me back into my subservient self again. There was no use in trying to feel worthy of praise. At every opportunity Isaac struck with a vengeance, demeaning me once again. He never stopped. What was the use of trying to see myself in a different light?

"I love you more than you love me," Isaac said.

He said these words, but he never showed his love. I made the big blunder of acknowledging my love in small ways, in my actions toward him.

Isaac was an introvert. I was an extrovert and a social person. We went to social events related to his job. That became my social life and I never complained. I was a marionette and Isaac held the cords. I felt like I was in a penitentiary. I was naïve and needed permission to do everything.

Isaac was emotionally abusive to my son Eugene. I had no one to talk to, so I talked to Eugene. We confided in each other. When he was in his teens our relationship was more like friends than mother and son. We trusted one another. I trusted Jude but she wasn't blood.

One day I went to see the movie *Exorcist* in Boston. It was troubling to me. It was about releasing an evil spirit that possessed a young girl's soul. I wasn't the only one disturbed by this movie. People with strong beliefs were shocked to see such a convincing movie.

The night I saw *Exorcist,* Isaac was working the night shift. After the movie it was time for bed. Strange sounds were coming from the walls: loud, heavy breathing that didn't go away. I panicked.

Isaac didn't like me to call him at work, but I did and said, "I'm terrified!"

Isaac said that the show had subliminal messages that were affecting other people and not to be concerned. But if you had the religious upbringing that I had, you would be more than worried!

After our conversation my anxiety subsided and I went to sleep. But I still wondered if this was only a subconscious communication or if there could have been another clarification. Might this sinister evil have been real? These were the thoughts going through my mind. Is it possible my mental illness was breaking through and I wasn't hearing voices, but sounds? I don't know. I have no crystal balls, just speculations.

Church played a large role in my life. As a child I was taught that the devil and his demons could take over my soul. I was indoctrinated with that belief. This is why I was upset about the terrible effect of the movie on me. It took a long time in therapy to erase this kind of thinking.

One night all the administrators and doctors, included Isaac and me, were invited to a banquet. We walked by a fountain in the entrance and one of the therapists teasingly asked, "Who's going to go swimming in the fountain tonight?"

That was a dare and I still had that daredevil nature in me. However, I would never disgrace my husband. I was sitting at the table with Isaac and his assistant Bea, who was seeing an anesthesiologist named Dave. We all had designated tables.

As far as Isaac was concerned Bea could do no wrong; she was perfect and it wasn't a secret. He told me this often and of course that made me feel worse about myself. I was the imperfect one, the stupid one, the ugly one. How could I match up to her? In his eyes it was impossible and so it was in my eyes as well.

I was drinking wine that night. Dave kept refilling my glass and asking, "What do I see in your eyes?" He repeated the same question with no response from me. "Tell me," he said. "I'm a doctor."

Dave was about to get a taste of what was in my eyes: mania. Madness wasn't too far behind. Dave looked like he was hypnotized. "I'll give you twenty dollars if you swim in the fountain," he said.

I replied no and he put twenty more into the pot. The daredevil in me, combined with the mania, was overpowering. This frog took her big leap! Off came the shoes. It was time to swim in the fountain.

My dress buttoned in the front, which made it easy to remove. This swan splashed in the fountain in panties and bra, did the breast stroke to the other side and back then stepped out. I started to button my dress. Isaac, Dave and Bea reappeared.

My dress wasn't buttoned all the way. Isaac commanded, "Give the money to Bea."

She never received any money from me. Dave pointed out, "Why should Bea receive the money? It was a dare between Susan and me. Susan did all the work and accomplished the bet so she has the money as far as this goes."

We entered the restaurant and no one knew what had happened because there were curtains over the windows and the fountain wasn't visible. My madness was just starting; this was just the icing on the cake. The way my mind was going anything was possible.

That night Dave called Isaac to apologize.

"There's no problem," Isaac simply replied. It was left like that. Isaac didn't have a problem with any of this. He liked my personality and sexiness. When someone was attentive to me he wasn't jealous, he liked the idea. *Isn't she wonderful,* he thought? I was all his but not all mine.

The next time we went to a party Dave was there again; I gave him a bottle. I had told him about my bottle digging and he said he'd like one of them. This already seemed familiar, giving an old bottle to a doctor.

I was unknowingly healing myself. Now he had a piece of me. I was suddenly appreciated. I felt special that he would want something like this from me.

Dave's girlfriend Bea was young and beautiful, but he always stared at *me*, as if bewitched. He was trying to figure out what fascinated him. I know what he saw in my eyes. It was a universe without end.

There were numerous times men have asked in amazement, "What do I see in your eyes?" They seemed compelled to vocalize this; what were these secrets my eyes held that pulled them as if they were drowning?

My eyes were a glimpse into my world, where there were no limits and I was the only one that could see beyond what the bottom held: pure ecstasy and feeling at one with the universe. Madness has its rewards.

I never complained about Isaac; he was a good provider. However, no one knew what he was really like in the home except my best friend Jude. Our biggest arguments were about me working and my friendship with Jude.

I had to fight to work part time. My husband thought differently; he was the provider and I was the Jewish wife and matriarch who should stay home taking care of him and the children.

The right to work was the only argument I ever won, but believe me winning was no easy task. Isaac was a shrewd opponent. I shattered his perfect world and refused to abide by his rules. He lost this battle, but there was a price to pay. Isaac often refused to talk to me, sometimes for as long as a week.

Yet when it came to working and keeping Jude as my friend, I fought like a vicious tiger. There had to be something that was *mine* and these two things were. I wasn't about to let them go without a fight.

Face-to-face verbal confrontations became common. Isaac screamed into my face and I screamed into his, but I did not budge. I told him I would work and I would keep my friend Jude. These were the only things that said I had value and they were there to stay.

Eugene played with boys in our neighborhood. I was suspicious about one boy who Eugene described as a much older person. When he expounded on the situation Isaac dismissed it but I was frightened. Isaac wasn't about to do anything about it so I found out where this man lived.

"I'm going to talk to him and if I am not back send in the police," I said.

I knocked on the man's door. He was at least six feet tall and about 22. I yelled with an angry voice, "You don't know me and I don't know you, but stay away from my son!"

Eugene was only six years old at the time, a handsome young child with deep brown eyes and beautiful blonde hair— a pedophile's dream.

Two days later, there was a knock on my door. Two detectives held a box full of photos of missing children. They started to ask Eugene questions.

Eugene said, "The man took a knife and held it over his head and then tried to put his hand down my pants but I started to cry and he stopped."

At that moment I wanted to kill Isaac! My son was almost a fatality. If I hadn't acted on my gut feelings he might be dead.

The case went to court and the pedophile was released on a technicality. Though the police broke in because they heard someone screaming, no one was found. Without a search warrant the evidence was dismissed. Though this happened forty years ago it seems like yesterday.

Jude wanted me to leave Isaac. "Jude, he's getting better," I said to her in a shaky voice, over and over.

This went on for years: "He's getting better." "He's getting better." "He's getting better."

Jude was my sounding board for fourteen years until 1989, when I had my psychotic break and the marriage disintegrated. This was my way out; I put him through hell and he divorced me. That was the first time I ever saw him cry. I was too far gone; no one could have lived with me in this condition.

I spent fourteen years married to Isaac. I was a good mother and a faithful wife. I did everything for my husband but throughout our entire marriage, Isaac never complimented me on anything. He did just the opposite.

I was insecure because of Bipolar Disorder and he fortified it. When I gained some self-respect he saw it and sent me to my knees. My submissive self reappeared and due to his heckling I disappeared.

I was like a prisoner in my own home, never going anywhere other than work. When people gave me a compliment, I was unable to respond with a thank you. I had such self-hatred inside I felt like raw hamburger.

I needed to fix my outside because my insides felt like an empty void filling with self-loathing. The outside was the only thing I could control. I made myself pretty and changed like a chameleon, satisfying everyone I came into contact with.

One time when Isaac and I went to a party a man asked Isaac, "How did you get such a beautiful wife?"

Could he be talking about me? *Yes,* I thought, *He could be talking about me.* The man only saw the outside, not the ugliness within.

After Isaac and I were married five years my repressed anger waited to strike. Isaac and I had arguments, but he did all the talking and refused to listen to my responses. They were one-sided disputes and I stuffed my anger. Yet I saw red; something malicious inside wanted control. During one argument, I unplugged the radio and in a fury sent it flying. Pieces soared everywhere. It landed on the floor and I crushed it into several fragments. The shattered glass was a fitting metaphor of what I had become.

When I broke things and Isaac didn't respond my rage turned inward. The rage increased when I bought Eugene a camcorder that cost $1,000.00. I was a dangerous volcano, building up with pressure, ready to burst at any moment. The next avenue was to take it out on myself.

Self-harm was born. I lost reality. I could take no more and finally I tried to commit suicide. I held a butcher knife over my head and aimed it at my left wrist.

Once again I was hospitalized in the psychiatric unit.

During this big break my head split in two. I was beyond psychotic; I crossed the line named "Insanity." I was lost, nowhere to be found, even to myself.

Meanwhile my son was in a hospital in Florida after attempting suicide; I thought I would lose my job because my stress and mental illness were becoming evident; my husband wanted a divorce; I wasn't getting any sleep and self-medicated with alcohol to help me sleep and lessen my severe mood swings. I was in the hospital for two and a half months.

Isaac visited with the children and screamed, "When are you coming home?"

It got to the point that staff had to speak to him about his behavior.

"Who is the crazy one here?" they asked in nasty voices.

After I was discharged from the hospital Isaac brought me home. He dropped me off like a hot potato and went to his parents' home in Rhode Island. I felt abandoned. He left me there alone, a suicidal wife. So much for support!

Isaac said, "There's nothing wrong with you."

He insisted that I get another opinion. I went to a psychiatrist in Boston and after only half an hour he confirmed the diagnosis of Bipolar Disorder. Still Isaac refused to accept his findings. It took twenty years before he said I was sick.

One day something inside of me snapped and I lost control of my sexuality. My sex drive was insatiable; I could have spontaneous climaxes at will. How crazy is this? I didn't even need a partner.

I found myself in an affair with Joseph, a good-looking man I worked with. My seductions began with him, but they did not end with him.

"Meet me in the basement: the tank room," he said. I decided to undress.

He liked what he saw and said, "Let's have a drink after work."

I put my clothes back on and replied, "Sure."

I had never been with anyone since Isaac. My sexual appetite was increasing at an astonishing rate.

If I was in my right mind my affair with Joseph would have never happened. I was as faithful as a dog in both of my marriages no matter how I was treated. But when I was psychotic my sexual appetite was out-of-sight.

I told Joseph, "Joseph, I'm going to take you where you've never been before." This was a statement I always used with him.

He said, "This is like being in a picture." He had something there. *Movie time!*

Joseph remarked, "Having sex with you is like another world!"

One occasion everyone at work went to a bar for a drink. Joseph and I sat together. At the far end of the bar sat a young man who strikingly resembled Tom Cruise. Well, that's all I had to see. I began flirting from the distance with him. Joseph became angry with my teasing; his jealousy was apparent. This was the last time we saw each other.

I thought if I told the truth about Joseph, my husband would forgive me. This backfired but I was so psychotic by this time, I was unable to lie. I blurted out whatever was on my mind, sometimes explicitly and told Isaac graphic details about my sexual encounters with Joseph.

Isaac was furious. He called Joseph and screamed obscenities.

Joseph replied, “It’s been over for a year.”

That was the end of the conversation. I never realized it but I’d wanted to hurt Isaac for his countless years of abuse. In reality I was incapable of hurting him.

Isaac stopped having sex with me and wanted a divorce. His pride stepped in the way of any reconciliation and he held me accountable for the rest of my life. I became a problem to Isaac. He didn't like to solve problems so I was in the way.

He refused to talk to me, even about our children, for many years. He believed people should never talk about bad things. I didn't understand this kind of thinking. I was quite the opposite. I want to solve problems as they arrive, otherwise they just get bigger and harder to solve.

Isaac never forgave me. We decided our children would live with him for two years and the next two years with me. This was the divorce order. It was grueling trying to visit my children. His bitterness always got in the way and the children often had to come between us.

When it was my time for my children to live with me, my illness made it impossible. *I* could hardly live at home. Finding a job in the hospital was too stressful. Because of my sickness, my children lived with their father until I could cope with the stress.

When Jack was seventeen my children came to live with me for ten years. All four had my genes and developed mental illness. To say their suffering was hell on wheels is an understatement. That story is a book in itself.

After the reprehensible affair Isaac finally initiated the divorce. By then I was too out-of-control for him to handle. The day we left the courthouse in 1989 was the first time I ever saw Isaac shed a tear.

I was given a choice at work to keep my hours or take a leave of absence. I took the leave of absence, which turned out to be a bad choice. When I went back to my job I was informed that I could not return until I stopped taking medication. I was ineligible for disability insurance by *two days*. Was I screwed or what?

It was a blessing for both Isaac and me that I became sick and had to walk the long and painful path to sanity. Otherwise I would not have left him and we would still be in this abusive marriage.

After the divorce I became homeless. In the divorce agreement I had agreed to find a job after two months but could not. The night two months was up I went to our bedroom and Isaac shouted, “Get off the property or I will call the police!”

My father knew the person I was; too kind and forgiving. He said to me in a very stern voice, “If that man ever comes to your door don’t let him in; remember what he did to you!”

I went to live with my sister and her family in Lincoln. I lived with her for two weeks. She helped me find a job and an apartment in nearby Woonsocket.

My sister bought me a gas stove for cooking and to heat my flat. It was the perfect stove. She was crucial in getting Eugene and me off the street, so it was imperative that I find a job. I was hired as a respiratory therapist at Traverous Pediatrics in Providence.

I felt that this was a turning point in my life. But I never should have had that job; I was out of my mind and dangerous for such a position. Looking back, it’s fortunate no harm came to anyone. Because I had worked so many years in hospitals, this job came easily for me.

Twenty years after our divorce when Isaac came over to see the boys, now men, I suggested, “Isaac, let’s go out to dinner.” He agreed.

That was a big surprise; I had been sure he would say no. In the restaurant I sat across from him and said, “I'm sorry for ruining your life.” I started to cry.

He replied, “You were sick and it wasn't your fault.”

I had waited twenty years to hear these words and used to say to myself, *I hope I live long enough to hear him say it wasn’t my fault and he forgives me.* Finally we forgave both each other and ourselves. It took time but we healed.

FACES IN THE DARKNESS

Aunt Mary and Uncle Brad lived close by. They were instrumental in one of the most traumatic, hurtful experiences of my life. Uncle Brad was a despicable human being; an unloving monster; a sociopath by nature. He had no heart and he had no remorse about inflicting pain on others, including me.

Aunt Mary didn't have these qualities, but she would not leave him nor report him to the authorities. She accepted and went along with this pathetic being.

Sometimes the enemy is within people that you love and trust, not a monster hiding in an alley. The dark days were about to begin with a vengeance. I didn't have the tools to retaliate, to save myself. I sunk into the quagmire as I tried to leap over the quicksand without getting swallowed whole. But I failed!

At age 19, childlike and senseless described my mind. My Aunt Mary and Uncle Brad took Eugene and me into their home. The town was familiar to me and I knew mostly everyone there. This made me feel safe, but I was in for a big shock. Unbeknownst to me, a snare was descending, ready to choke the life force out of me.

My Uncle Brad paid the moving bill. What a big mistake! I had no money to pay him back and I felt like I owed him something. As my father would say, "You don't get something for nothing." Right on the money, dad.

But it wasn't money that my Uncle Brad wanted; he had different plans. It's hard to talk about my uncle's actions and my reactions. I'm ashamed about the part I played in this, the guilt of just being there. Was I at fault for planting the seed?

Feeling the victim again, Susan? How are you going to get out of this one? You're not!

When something bad happened to me I'd say, "It's not happening."

I felt like a bug in a spider's web; I couldn't fight. This was detachment. While being sexually abused as a young child, I learned to be the wire-trapped bug that the spider twists round and round in its silky web. This mindset lasted many years until I got professional help.

On Friday nights around 10 o'clock my Uncle Brad went out for pizza and beer. There was always pizza and alcohol. My aunt said, "Susan, when you're married for long time, you have to dress up in different costumes and dance for your husband."

I never heard of such things. I was only nineteen and they were trying to involve me in their sex life. One Friday night she dressed up as a belly dancer with twirly things on her nipples. She did a seductive dance and invited me to dance with her.

Something seemed odd about all this, yet familiar. I felt obligated to them for taking me in, so I played along, never imagining what would happen next.

When I was twelve, I visited my Aunt Mary and Uncle Brad often; they lived down the street from me. Aunt Mary was a great seamstress and made me clothes. Mom and dad didn't have the money to buy new clothes. I always had hand-me downs and shoes with cardboard covering up holes in their soles.

My Aunt Mary and Uncle Brad were only in their twenties at the time. I remember the music playing and my aunt telling me to dance with my uncle.

He whispered in my ear, "I can't wait until you're eighteen."

At times when Uncle Brad was lying on the couch without a shirt, Mary said, "Sit on your uncle's lower back and give him a backrub."

So I did. Something seemed improper about this. I was confused; I was only twelve!

My uncle Brad was drinking the night he raped me, but being drunk is no justification for his actions. My son was sick that evening and slept with me. We were sleeping when my uncle pushed my knees to my chest and entered me.

Then I woke up. My aunt called his name; she was just down the hall.

I said in a whisper, "Please get off of me! Don't rouse my son!"

Thank God Eugene never woke up during this vicious act! It would've scarred him for life.

Softly I said, "Uncle Brad, Aunt Mary will overhear."

Then I blacked out. I don't remember him getting off me. It's as if I died at that moment. I don't remember anything more about the attack I experienced that night. Maybe that's a good thing, to not remember, just another door slammed shut in the dark hallways of my mind.

Door slamming didn't end there. The keys hung on the doorknobs for many years. Some were opened, some remained closed. The child in a woman's dress emerged slowly, growing up, but still childlike. After two decades my throbbing recollections diminished, but the anger stayed.

Life is no longer a creepy movie. I dealt with these memories and emotions. But one monster was not forgotten.

My family doctor stole my innocence when I was only four and I wanted it back. But Uncle Brad's assault was too severe to remain silent. I told Mother the specifics about the rape. She was livid, furious and wanted to kill.

I said, "Mom, don't tell Aunt Mary."

But she did. Yet even after the news about the rape, my aunt would not leave him. It was inconceivable. Why did she stay? What else had he done that she had no knowledge of? And what was in the future? Who would be his next victim?

My aunt didn't have a visible mental illness, but mom said she talked to her dead mother. That wasn't enough to diagnosis a mental illness. But she might have been a bit touched.

Leaving my aunt and uncle's home wasn't easy. Fury wasn't present at first; I was in shock. Denial also played a part, denial of the violence by someone I trusted, a loved one. And it was my entire fault because I was there.

This doesn't make any sense now, but that was the way I felt then. I carried that burden and belief system for many years.

I didn't have a therapist when I was nineteen and the next best thing was a priest. He advised me to get out and get out fast and I did just that. My spirit and state of mind were broken almost beyond restoration.

My mom said, "Confront your uncle."

Confronting my abuser with anger and determination worked. At that moment, I was no longer The Victim.

"You could have gotten me pregnant!" I shouted to my uncle with an outcry of hate that vibrated from within.

It was so loud he must have wanted to block his ears. He said, "I used a condom."

He used a condom... how considerate.

That's all he said, in a voice with no emotion. And he left it like that. How cold. My words of outrage didn't concern him at all. He just dismissed it, like it never happened. That he had nothing more to say made me feel dirty.

I went into the bathroom and scrubbed my skin. I tried to shed like a snake and grow new skin, clean and fresh. I immersed myself in soapy water trying to get his filth off of me. I scrubbed and scraped and scoured, trying to wash away the memories. The world was a scary place. Between my family and my doctor, the monsters I saw as a child were materializing.

I wondered about the transformation in my demeanor. Mom said, "It's all right to get angry."

My childish behavior left and a tiger was born. But recollections lingered. Four words stayed stuck to my tongue: *"MY UNCLE RAPED ME!"*

There was no closure then or now and only a tiny place inside me for forgiveness. I told myself, *After this, no one will make me cry.*

When my aunt was sixty she had a heart transplant. I called her and to my surprise my uncle Brad was on the line.

I hadn't talked to them for thirty years. "Your actions have crippled me for years," I said to him. "Aren't you at least sorry?"

He said, "I don't want to open Pandora's Box."

After all those years, still no closure. He just didn't give a shit; he was unrepentant. I had waited all those years… and what did I expect? Possible change of heart? Or did he even have a heart? If he did, he didn't share this with me.

I don't practice any organized religion. But I do believe in God. I certainly am not perfect and would like to be forgiven for the things I have done. So my head says to forgive my uncle, but my heart says something else.

He was sick in a different way than me. So I forgave him, but it was difficult to do because he had no remorse, not even "I'm sorry."

The only revenge is if there is a God, my uncle will pay for what he did.

I buried my emotions behind a brick wall and the mortar hardened. Later in life I took it down, but could only face one brick at a time. It was too painful. One brick only, or the wall would crush me and the bad memories would overwhelm me all at once. This I could not bear. If the wall came down all at once I'd be in an asylum sitting in a rocking chair, rocking back and forth forever.

You would think by that time I hated men. I was the most trusting yet non-trusting person imaginable and a glutton for punishment. Giving up was not in my vocabulary. So I repeated one abusive relationship after another.

My middle name was chaos, a familiar state of mind, a means of detachment. Living in a state of chaos was an escape from reality and facing the past. Even the moment was too painful to conceive. Turmoil was familiar and if there was none, I found a way to bring it home.

In this mindset I didn't deal with anything. Recovery would wait a long time. I had yet to face all the nightmares in my life. It's hard to believe my own story but it's all true—for me, peace wasn't to be the case.

One day Dave, a friend from Eugene's workplace, asked me to his house for dinner. I saw no reason why I shouldn't go, no danger.

There was no reason to think he'd rape me. He was in his twenties, I was in my forties, it was implausible. I was old enough to be his mother. He was handsome and could have any girl he wanted. He didn't have a mental illness in his way, but I certainly did.

He made swordfish and we both had a piece. It was quite tasty. Then he invited me into his bedroom, which he said he had remodeled.

He said, "Susan, come and see the work I've had done. The layout, furniture and the colors of the walls are magnificent."

Unthinking as usual, I entered his bedroom. He gave me a quick hard shove and I landed on the bed. He raped me, but I put up a damn good fight.

I managed to slap him in the face as hard as I could and it seemed to stun him. I was able to escape only because he wasn't a big man. If he was, I would have lost.

I ran out of there as fast as I could. I had only twenty minutes to get to work. I kept thinking, *I'm the only one covering the third shift. I have to relieve the second shift or they'll have to work another 12 hours.*

It's hard to believe that I worked the whole night after being raped, but I did. This was partly because I shut down emotionally and partially because I was taking a strong central nervous system depressant. I had a very flat affect and a deadpan face that showed no emotion; I was unable to smile. I was not there.

The next day I reported the rape to the police. They didn't believe me. I took a lie detector test and the needle went off the chart. I passed with flying colors.

One police officer said, "Susan, you sure like them young."

At that moment I saw red, but there was nothing I could do or say. I had passed the lie detector test and I had told the truth. Yet the officer was insinuating that I was the problem.

Dad advised, "Don't go to trial. Let it go. This will only make you sick. It's too much stress. There is a report on file at the police station if he does it again."

So I listened to Dad, knowing they would pull up my past and make me the guilty one. That's the way they look at rape. Not just the man is on trial; the woman is also. Did she entice him? What was she wearing? Dad was right again. Let it go!

STRANGE BEDFELLOWS

My mood changed and I became flirtatious as I approached one of the men. This was not unusual behavior for manic-me. He said no to my suggestion, which I am sure was sexual. I'd done this before and I didn't want to continue. But did I have a choice? NO!

I can understand why restraining orders are issued; I have firsthand experience with obsession, but a heightened form, connected to madness. Sexual obsession is relentless, a pursuit with no boundaries, just full steam ahead with no brakes.

BURT

Severe mania and depression wouldn't hit me hard until seventeen years later. That is when sexual cravings and desires beyond the imagination tormented me. This perpetual sexual aching resembled a male teenager constantly unable to control his erection.

What a nightmare this out of control sexual appetite was! I had a flirtatious personality and I wasn't ugly. This gave me the pick of the crop, with no problem finding sex partners.

Whoever I liked always liked me. That was no big surprise; I was a magnet and pulled everyone to me. They got caught in my web; it was hard to break free from manic me.

Burt was my first conquest. He was thirty-four and I was twenty. I have no recollection where we met. His ethnic background was French and he was a carpenter by trade. Burt had a twelve year old son from his first marriage; he was separated and filing for divorce. I was sure he still loved her. He was having a hard time letting go, until he met me. He was falling in love with a child in a woman's dress, me!

At twenty my sexuality was pretty straight-laced. Burt was fourteen years older than me and more experienced in sexual matters. He had an understanding about life that I didn't possess.

I wasn't fully driven by my illness yet. Madness had a mind of its own and was waiting for the right moment to pop it ugly head. If I was ill this wouldn't bother me—ass licking that is—but that was nothing compared to what I was capable of doing under the influence of madness.

When I lived in a small apartment in Central Falls, Rhode Island. Burt visited me every night, even though he lived in Providence. He would bring Delmonico steak, cook it and then pour vinegar over it. This seemed strange, but I decided to try it and found it quite tasty. This steak was very expensive; nothing but the best for me. I was on welfare at the time and couldn't afford expensive steak.

Burt and I never went to movies or family gatherings. It was mostly watching television, eating, and sex; this was an unpromising pattern throughout our relationship. There were no long intense conversations. What do you expect? I was still a bubblegum chewer, a kid. I can still see Burt sitting in an overstuffed chair in my living room when I told him that our relationship was over.

In a soft tone of voice I said, “Burt, I’ve met someone else.”

His head went down and in a sad tone of voice he said, “I want to marry you.”

I told him, “No, it's over.”

He left but came back the next day. Now the pressure was on him.

In a little boy’s voice he said, “Please, please, I beg you don’t leave me.”

Within that moment I turned into a statue, unable to move. What was happening to me? I sensed an absence of my awareness but I was determined to end this relationship. Was I catatonic? I couldn't lift my arm. I panicked. My mind snapped.

With a deliberate high pitched scream I yelled “No!”

Then I started to move. I asked myself, *What was that?* After that he left and I never saw him again.

WALTER/TIM

Walter was twenty-eight and I was twenty-one when we met at the hospital. He came from a Communist Country and that he would tell me how he escaped someday, but that day never came. He said the peanuts that we were eating were a luxury in his country and they would have to stand in line all day to buy some.

He wanted to become a psychiatrist and he asked me to go out dancing one evening. We listened to the music more than we danced. He wasn’t the dancing type but I was a dancing fool.

I had very low self-esteem due to my mental illness. I remember asking my mother, “Why would a doctor want to go out with me?”

I don't know what my mother's response was but it was positive.

My position as assistant chief of the respiratory helped but not enough to reverse this kind of thinking.

On one date, Walter took me to a New York City play called *Old Calcutta* that was banned in Boston because of nudity. Of course this was forty years ago. How silly that would be today!

We went to the Olive Tree Cafe in Greenwich Village, where they served only tea and coffee, no alcohol. There were tables upstairs to play a game of chess.

The basement floor had many tables with only small walking spaces between tabletops. This limited the space for a dance floor. The music was intoxicating. There were mandolins, bass instruments and a singer that sang in different languages. There was a diversity of people in the room, with outfits ranging from rags to expensive furs.

I was getting high on the music, and the atmosphere took me to a heightened level of awareness. I was experiencing low levels of mania. That is all I needed; I was about to fly!

A man with a big belly and a handkerchief in his hand started to dance in the aisle. He wasn't a very handsome man, but his dancing was still seductive. This caught my eye. I was already high on the music and started to dance with him in the aisle. Now that I was involved, his dancing was becoming erotic in nature. We were like two birds flying, doing a mating love dance, caught in the moment, both electrified.

This memory still remains so vivid in my mind. The air was filled with electricity and so was I, one hundred lightning bolts all at once. There was an explosion! Energy burst. Every pore ignited with flames that lit the room because I was on fire with my chemically charged brain.

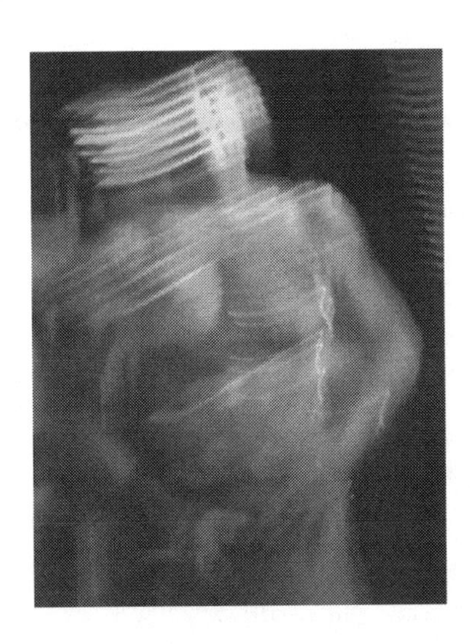

Walter was so kind to patients, not like some of the American doctors. He always commented on my smile. "You're always smiling, Susan. People that frown will wear it on their faces as they get older."

Before long, you guessed it, we were seeing each other. He lived with six interns on the hospital grounds in a house called The Brown House. I don't remember the color of the house; it could have been brown. There was another doctor that had his eye on me so to speak. But I wasn't that kind of person to go out with two people at a time.

When we got to his apartment we had a sexual encounter. Walter said, "Susan, thank you for sleeping with me because I know it was only to please me."

He was right. He cared about me but we weren't madly in love with each other.

Later I was on the bed, naked, lying face-down. Walter said, "Susan, you look like you're sixteen, your body is beautiful."

I was twenty-one at the time and took this as a nice compliment.

Walter bought a new car, a Volvo. We went for many long rides, especially on the beach.

One day we went to the dunes where no one could see us. The heat from the sun was beating down my back, making a puddle of sweat on his lower abdomen. I still remember sweat trickling down my body as it met his. I was on fire with the heat and intensity of the moment.

At that moment I didn't exist. I was surrounded by ecstasy and so was he. I wasn't manic but I am sure he didn't forget this moment and neither would I.

One day I telephoned Walter from work and asked him to bring me my underwear that I had left behind at his apartment. A woman overheard and criticized my behavior.

My response was, "If I go out with cats, dogs, or another woman, it's none of your business."

As you can see I was quite colorful even then. After that there was no response from her. Anyway, who could reply to that?

Walter told me, "Susan, don't fall in love with me."

I said, "I won't."

I said to myself, *I'll see someone else. This will help me so Walter will not be number one in my life.* I would have another distraction, another man.

I started to see Tim, an oncologist. Tim's wife had died of breast cancer about two years prior. His house was right near the water in Warwick, Rhode Island. Tim was fifty-six and I was twenty-one.

I noticed him right away when I was behind him in the chow line. He was quite tall and handsome with a very lean muscular build. I said to myself, *Yummy, yummy and yummy!*

In a deep voice he said, "Hello Susan, how about lunch?"

My response of course was yes. That was no big surprise; I was a big magnet and pulled everyone to me. They got caught in my web; it was hard to break free from manic me.

Tim was a smooth character but kind. My father would say this guy was a fox; he was older and wiser, so able to influence me.

However, he was not the type to use a woman. He was a gentleman who would not exploit me. He saw a beautiful, young, sexy lady and scooped her up. Being with him was a good experience; he treated me like a lady, though I was neither sophisticated nor a lady.

Tim lived near Warwick Golf Club. It was quite close to the ocean. We had a lot of fun together. One time we were sitting in his giant bathtub. He scooped his two hands around my breasts.

"How beautiful," he said. "You're just so perfect." I can still feel his hands caressing them.

When I was twenty one, but my body was sixteen. Childbirth never changed my appearance; it was as if I had never given birth. I was the same as my mother, never a stretch mark or widening of the hips.

Tim had a king-size bed. I worked very hard to satisfy him. He always had a good disposition. It was easy to be with him; we liked and respected each other. This was no romantic love affair. He got what he needed and I got what I wanted. It was a symbiotic relationship.

We spent a lot of time at his house, which had a beautiful fireplace. We had dinner dates; sex; and Courvoisier, the best, most expensive brandy. We listened to classical music as we sipped fine brandy from a glass snifter.

When the brandy got to the bottom of the glass my nose got in the way. I had to tip the glass almost upside down to drink the rest. I had an Italian nose, not big, not small, but somewhere in-between. My lips and eyes were also big and this compensated for my nose.

When Tim and I went to Chinatown I picked out a new outfit, black and white pants with a red shirt (How gaudy!). I was definitely not sophisticated at the time; in time I would learn how to dress stylishly, instead of sexily. Coming from a blue-collar family, I didn't know on which side of the plate the fork and knife should go and I still don't.

The restaurant was Chinese and so was everyone there. One of the dishes was a big fish. Its eye seemed to be staring at me.

We came back from Chinatown in his Porsche at speeds up to one hundred miles per hour. Was I having fun? You bet!

Then we moved to the bed. The love making was like floating on a cloud; was it our love making, brandy or both? My lips were big and puffy. My skin was soft and supple and smooth as a baby's ass. My eyes were like deep wells that had no bottom; look into them and you were lost.

I was quite the package. Tim bought me diamonds, earrings and a gold bracelet. Later in life I would drop them in my sink by accident. I seemed to have an affinity for losing these items or misplacing them.

I wasn't the only woman Tim was seeing. Kimmy was a nurse in her forties from Rhode Island Hospital that he saw occasionally. She was possessive and more desperate than me. I was only twenty-one; I had time on my side. Hers was running out.

When she found I was seeing Tim she became unraveled. It was frightening. She was more than furious—try violent and homicidal. She was some scary creature; her eyes were on fire. She was about to light him up.

One early morning we were sipping on our drinks, brandy if you can believe it. There was a knock on the door and Kimmy flew in like a bat out of hell. She took the drink from his hand and threw what was left in his face. She hit him with an open hand, a devastating blow to the face, leaving a bright red glow.

Then she took off in a flash and went to his bedroom. She cut his electric blanket with a pair of scissors. I think she was trying to electrocute him.

What else could this be? She ran down the stairs, flew out the door and slammed it behind her. Tim couldn't apologize enough for this behavior.

With a soft compassionate voice I said, "I have no problem with this. She's not mad at me. She's taking her anger out on you. I am not jealous of her and I won't stay away because of this."

I left the relationship shortly after so I am not sure what happened between them. But I am sure Tim's charm won her back—or he put a restraining order on her! I hope everything worked out well for Tim.

Walter discovered the extent of our relationship when the calves of my legs were painful and Tim examined me, finding phlebitis in both legs, and admitted me to the hospital. I spent fourteen days there. Of course, he was an oncologist and it made no sense that a doctor who treated cancer patients would do this kind of admission.

The phlebitis was due to birth control pills. I had to stop them, then pregnancy would become an issue.

On the Chinese New Year and Tim came into my hospital room. I wasn't expecting him. He had a flask of brandy and two glasses with him. We both had a glass and toasted in the New Year. Can you imagine bringing alcohol into the hospital and sharing it with your patient? Good thing he didn't go to court; sometimes alcohol and medications don't mix. However, he knew just one drink wasn't going to harm me.

On the grand-rounds, doctors and interns went from patient to patient and looked over the charts. Once Walter came to my room, he saw Doctor Tim Kong on my chart and put two and two together. He knew beyond a shadow of a doubt I was seeing Dr. Kong. Yes, I was dating them both at the same time. I was not the type to date two people at once but these were different circumstances.

Walter was furious and when we saw each other again, I saw Doctor Kong's head carved in the bedpost. Boy was I shocked! I had some clarifying to do. I was unable to get out of this one but I sure tried, with little results in my favor. However, Walter played a part in this triangle and needed to share some responsibility for what was happening.

"You said 'Don't love me' so I went out with Tim," I said. "Walter, it's not my fault. You were asking for it and I gave it to you."

This was not an angry remark, just the truth.

Walter said, "I want to marry you."

This was after he found out that I was seeing Doctor Kong. His words were not coming from his heart; or from being madly in love with me. That I am sure of.

I said, "You don't love me, it's your pride that hurts."

He even wanted to buy me a diamond.

"I will stop seeing Tim. And keep your diamond. I don't want one," I said.

Tim was disappointed, but he understood. He was a man of the world, so to speak. I am sure this situation had passed him already, maybe more than once. He took the news in stride.

After that, maybe six months passed. Then I found the man I was to marry. I was in the hospital when I spotted Tim in the corridor. I told him the news.

He said in a sad voice, "Don't get married," and kissed me.

His concern wasn't about losing me; it was about nailing this tiger's paw to the floor.

Marriage would turn out to be a torture chamber, a cage I couldn't break free of, fourteen years in a marriage that would swallow me.

Walter was doing his internship in psychiatry at Belleview Hospital in New York City. The next time I saw Walter he seemed disturbed and close to tears. A patient had died and Walter thought he had given a patient too much medication.

But I think that may not have been the case. Forty years ago medication was a crap shoot, just like today and had devastating side effects—even sudden death. The side effect of the medication could have been the cause of death, not too much medication.

Walter was a very compassionate person and I felt so sorry for him. He was human; we all make mistakes. If only Walter knew this information back then, it would have saved him some pain. He could have thought it sudden death, which could be the side effect.

I took a plane from Green Airport in Providence to JFK Airport in New York. I took the subway and ended up in Harlem on New Year's Eve of 1970. I stuck out like a sore thumb; everyone was black except me.

I needed directions to Belleview Hospital where Walter was staying. A very nice man gave me directions and God is the only one who knows how I got to my destination, but I did.

I flew to New York every other weekend to see Walter after he moved, but as time passed we saw less and less of each other. One time I came to see him with a huge hickey on my neck. I had the balls to show up in this condition! Don't get me wrong, I didn't have sex with the man involved; he was a coworker and that night he was teaching me algebra for a course I was taking. He was my friend and it just happened. Of course he wanted more but I said no; that's the total truth.

Even after I explained, Walter was grumbling, "American girls. They'll bring you diseases."

We still saw each other but it was starting to slowly go downhill. He had bigger plans for himself and I wasn't in them. This relationship was going nowhere and it was about time to part.

The last time we saw each other; he'd applied for a fellowship as a sergeant in California and was to leave soon. It was a cold January night. He had on a gray overcoat and his shiny thick black hair was full of snowflakes.

This is the last thing I remember. I was sad to see him leave. I thought I would never see or hear from him again and I was right. Now that we have such great technology I was able to find Walter by internet in 2012, about forty years later.

He said in a soft tone, "Susan, I remember you. You were so nice. You were always smiling. I am sixty-eight now . . . Where did the time go? So are you looking up your lost flames for your book?"

I said, "No, I was just thinking of you and decided to look you up."

He was in the service for twenty years and when he left he became a neurologist. He was married but sounded somber and sad; sometimes we make mistakes when are young.

He was hesitant when I asked him if he had children. He paused for a moment and said nothing, so I didn't push the subject. Walter seemed unhappy about how his life turned out. He said he was to retire in two years at seventy.

Don't we all think the grass is greener? If he married me, a crazy out-of-control wife and a ticking time bomb, the explosion may have ruined his life completely. Marriage would have been a disaster.

SAJAAD

In 1970 I started to see Sajaad, a doctor from India. He was not the best lover I'd ever had; he sucked on my skin leaving many blue marks all over my body. I looked like a Dalmatian dog with spots all over. Their spots were black but mine were blue.

The only reason I saw him was because someone had to replace Walter. I always jumped from one relationship right into another, because I couldn't deal with being alone and addressing my past and present.

Because of the blood clots in my legs I could no longer take birth control pills. I told Sajaad about this but he disregarded it completely. To this day I have no idea why he did this. Was he that selfish and just didn't give a damn? He sure wasn't in love with me.

After two weeks my breasts hurt and my worst fears came true. Shortly after that I was admitted to the hospital for fourteen days with another diagnosis of phlebitis and blood clots again in my calves. I was put on a Heparin drip and on release switched to Coumadin, an oral medication. I found out later that this would cause bleeding in the newborn's brain and severe brain damage.

I told the horrifying news of the pregnancy to Sajaad. With a stern voice I said, "I will not marry you and I need an abortion."

He had no outward emotions that I could see about my condition. The doctors were afraid for my life because pregnancy contributed to the blood clotting.

I remained on Coumadin, a pill that thins the blood. Bloodwork was needed to monitor the clotting factor. I stopped taking the pills five days before the selected abortion date so I would not hemorrhage.

Abortion clinics were just starting. The back-alley butchers were disappearing when abortions became legal. It couldn't have started soon enough for me and other women in my position. The only abortion clinic was in New York City and I lived in Rhode Island. I had plans to drive myself to the clinic. How crazy was this?

I don’t know if Sajaad even knew I was in the hospital at this time, though he was an intern there. Even if he knew I doubt he would have visited me there. I wasn't in love with him and I wouldn't want him for a friend. As far as I was concerned he couldn't be trusted.

After the abortion he knocked at my door. He had the nerve to ask me out for a date. He gave me money to pay for the abortion.

I yelled, “Get out of my house!”

He was reluctant to leave. I told him, “If you don't leave now I’ll call the police.”

That was the last time I saw him. Sajaad was not his real name; his real name I have not forgotten. He probably moved on and went back to India. Every time I see a young woman from India I think, this could have been my daughter. For some reason I feel in my gut the baby would have been a girl.

THE TUG BOAT CAPTAIN

Just in time an intern introduce me to a tug boat captain who looked like Burt Reynolds. We started dating and made plans to go to New Jersey, where his parents lived.

We traveled to New Jersey to see his parents. His dad was a fisherman. They were very nice people.

I had the weekend off so in the morning Bob and I sailed with his father and picked up lobster traps. I saw a seal pop his head from the water. Later that evening we had fresh lobster and crab for dinner. It was absolutely delicious. We left Sunday night because I worked Monday morning. His mother wasn’t old fashioned so we slept in the same bed that night before we left.

I blurted out, “I can't see you next week. I’m pregnant and I’m driving myself to New York City for an abortion.”

He responded, “I’ll drive you there.”

And he did.

There were no problems going to the city and we found the abortion clinic without delay. I had to fill out forms before they would take me as their patient. There was one stumbling block and it was the Coumadin I was taking. They were afraid of hemorrhaging because one of the side effects of Coumadin was bleeding.

I told them, “I stopped taking the medication five days prior like you prescribed; what’s the big problem?” They were still reluctant to take me, but after some deliberation I was accepted.

They wheeled me into the operating room on a gurney. There was some conversation, but I can't remember what it was. A butterfly needle was put into my vein and then the countdown started. Ninety-nine, ninety-eight and the operation began.

I was brought up Catholic, so I believed the notion that I was taking a life. Yes, murder. I felt I had no choice but to have that abortion.

As I left the operating room, a tear came trickling down my face and I said, "God forgive me for what I have done."

Later I was told the child would have had severe birth defects because of the bleeding. I wish I could say that was the reason I took the baby's life but it wasn't. So now I became the monster that killed a living thing. The guilt and shame would stay with me for many years.

When we left the clinic my tug boat captain said, "The car has been impounded and the ticket is fifty dollars. I lost track of the time and the meter ran out."

We picked up his car on the waterfront from a dingy dirty place with a large gate around all the cars and a junkyard dog.

We found a hotel for the night and then left in the morning. I was still bleeding and thought I couldn't get pregnant and wasn't worried about infection. I had intercourse that night. I can't imagine what I was thinking to have sex right after surgery. I wasn't thinking!

I didn't get pregnant that night; however he would have been happy if I did.

Later in the relationship the tug boat captain asked me to marry him and even bought me a diamond, but I said that I had met someone else and I was going to marry him. He asked that I not tell anyone, saying, "I've never asked anyone to marry me before."

The look on his face was hurt and sad all at the same time. So I kept his secret until now. If I have any regrets it was not saying yes to his proposal. I always called him "the tug boat captain." I can't remember his name.

SETH

I needed someone as crazy as me, having the same intense desires. We found each other when he was twenty five and I was thirty seven. He said no one could keep up with him but he met his match. I called him the sex machine and he called me love goddess. This relationship lasted six years, but this need for constant sex would torment me for two and a half decades.

But there would be no restraining order on me. The person I was stalking was stalking me: Seth. Yes, we were both crazy at the time. How lucky could I be, having a person feeling the same about me as I did him? We could not get enough of each other. Even on the phone we felt we were inside each other.

If it was anyone else they would not want anything to do with me. I would not be able to stop and my aggressive behavior would push into calling the person nonstop, or approaching him, even with a restraining order on me.

Jail would not be a deterrent. The police would have to put me in shackles and handcuff me screaming all the way to jail. Having a mental illness would not save me; one year in the slammer would be my fate. That's why Seth was important, keeping me from jail.

"Are you still in there?" my son Michael curiously asked.

He was only ten years old. Was I a mother who subjected him to puzzling conduct with Seth behind the bedroom door? I am repulsed and sickened revealing this story. Not obvious to me, I thought this was normal, yes! Still married, not yet divorced. My children and Michael say they don't remember this today. How lucky am I they don't remember this. ***Mother?*** *Monster was a more fitting name. I can't question it happened****. I want to scream NO!***

When I lived in Northampton with Seth and his Uncle Bert, I was searching for a respiratory job in the Berkshires. I remember my interview at a North Adams nursing facility. I didn't say much to the head of the respiratory department, I just laid my resume down on his desk.

He began to read it and when he was finished he asked, "You want the job?"

Of course I said yes. Most of my adult life, I had worked in teaching hospitals in Boston. My résumé was impeccable, with 20 years of experience.

It was time to leave Northampton and get an apartment closer to work. I didn't have a car and needed to be in walking distance. Seth and I went to an auction and I picked up an antique table for our new apartment and chairs, a couple of mirrors and a small sofa. We rented a truck and Seth moved all the furniture; there was a lot of heavy lifting. At one point he wanted to get something to drink at a grocery store.

When we came out he started walking away from the truck. I called "Come back here, where are you are going?"

He kept walking and didn't respond. I was hysterical from pleading with him. Maybe something I said made him turn around and come back to the truck.

I noticed the phone was still functioning. I made a short call to the electric company and Seth made a call to a friend.

I unplugged the phone and as I was putting it away he said in a stern voice, "Give me the phone! I need to pay for the call."

I tried to explain that there was no problem and refused. He tackled me to the floor, threw me in the bed, tied my wrists with lamp wires to the bedposts and put a sock in my mouth.

Throughout my book I say I had no fear but this incident was different. I remember a tear in my right eye cascading downward over my cheek, landing on my chin. This was: the first time I experienced extreme fear in my entire life.

I could hear Seth from the other room talking on the phone.

Seth said softly, "I will pay for the phone call."

The voice on the other end replied, "No problem sir."

Immediately after that he entered the bedroom; and he looked down at me and said, "My God, I would never do this to you."

He proceeded to untie me and he took the sock out of my mouth but it wasn't over. As he walked into the living room he took his shirt off: I even remember it was yellow. Then he tied it around my neck. Was he going to strangle me?

I stood up to him. I put my finger to his chest and in an angry voice I said, "Take that shirt from my neck. I'm not afraid of you."

He removed it. I took full advantage of that slight moment of clarity. I slipped into the bedroom where there was a second phone and called the police.

When Seth saw the police he was able to pull it together and sound normal (whatever that is). He could always muster up some kind of sanity when seeing an official, especially the police.

The police took Seth to the emergency room at North Adams Regional Hospital to be evaluated. I was in the waiting room and all of a sudden I heard so much commotion.

Seth was out-of-control. He was put in four-point restraints and given a shot of Haldol. They took him by ambulance to a hospital in Chicopee; North Adams psychiatric ward could not handle someone as violent as Seth.

When I entered the hospital to visit Seth, a young, healthy and strong-looking fellow came over to me and exclaimed, "How do you handle him? It took six guys to hold him down!"

I replied, "As my dad would say, 'Susan you are Igor and Seth is the monster'."

When we reached the apartment, with no hesitation he moved the furniture into it. Though it was a small apartment it suited me fine. There were mostly elderly people living there. A big plus was there was a swimming pool.

When we reached the apartment, with no hesitation he moved the furniture into it. Though it was a small apartment it suited me fine. There were mostly elderly people living there. A big plus was there was a swimming pool. All the furniture was successfully placed in order. I had two phones; one in the bedroom and one in the kitchen.

Seth was over six feet tall. His physique was incredible; he was built like a brick shit house. Though he was usually handsome, when psychotic he was a scary-looking character. He was like Dr. Jekyll and Mr. Hyde. I never knew what to expect. He could be sweet and calm, then without warning turn into the monster.

Knowing all this, I should've been prepared for what happened one day. Seth became psychotic and whirled about the room talking in an English accent, though he was of German descent. He grabbed hold of me and for no particular reason, tossed me across the room into a chair.

It fell against the door, making a big dent. I will never forget this day that he was so irrational and threatening. My therapist had said Seth was a dangerous man and right about now her words were ringing in my ears.

He came to the chair where I was sitting and put his hands around my neck; *Oh Christ is he going to strangle me?* He released his grip around my neck, leaving bruises. He picked me up under my shoulders and threw me again.

This time I hit the couch, not a good landing. My arm hit a lamp and it went flying. *He's going to kill me.* He was not suicidal anymore, he was homicidal and I was the object of his fury.

As soon as this started it stopped. He probably wasn't taking his medication as he usually did. When he was on his medication he was gentle as a pussycat. Eventually it was mandatory that he take his medication and this behavior ceased.

Seth's mom is a classy lady; we have kept in touch all these years. Jasmine lives in California and comes east to see friends and Seth. In April of 2013 she invited Luke and me to dinner at the Whitley Inn, where she and her husband Bill were staying. Seth would not come to dinner and made unreasonable demands. He said he wasn't ready for a visit. My heart bleeds for this woman, never to see him reach reality, *Stuck in Never-Never Ever-Ever Land!*

Seth still has a piece of my heart. Yes, he was a nightmare, but he listened to my pain when no one would give me the time of day. We loved each other, psychotic style.

LILY

I met Lily on New Year's Eve of 1990 on the Rhode Island waterfront where I frequented the local bars and nightclubs. My mind so clearly remembers that day, I actually see the jam-packed bar I went to. A tall blonde fellow named Kirk started a conversation with me. He was a very lean, soft-spoken and handsome writer. He was visiting from Australia and would soon return.

He told me when he was young he slept with men and now slept with women. After Kirk said that, I became alarmed about sleeping with him, because AIDS was in the forefront. In its early stages it was a killer that only involved homosexuals, who the public thought were expendable. When the heterosexual population became affected research was introduced with the focus of a vaccine or medications to eradicate AIDS or put it into remission.

My newfound friend from Australia and I left the bar then strolled about the streets where stores sold their goods. There was free food, drink and fireworks (which were legal back then) for everyone.

Kirk said he was so happy that his relationship with an incredible athlete was over. He wanted to sleep with me; I said no but didn't explain why.

Actually the information that he used to sleep with men frightened me. He also said he'd slept with a friend who'd had a mastectomy as his way of comforting her about her deformity; being an author he recited a beautiful comforting poem to her. I can't remember the verses, only the feelings of inner harmony that it echoed. I didn't know how to respond, so just listened.

It was time to go dancing. There was a long line but it moved quickly. Before I knew it we were inside. The bar contained mostly women. I had no idea it was a gay bar until a pretty woman of twenty-one asked me to dance.

I didn't see anything unusual about this. I was fascinated by this place with such friendly people. The pulsating music was great for dancing; every song was just right. I surely would be going back there.

Dancing was my major coping mechanism and this was certainly the place to be. The last dance with Lily was a slow dance, then she asked me if I would have dinner with her at an Italian restaurant in Federal Hill.

I still didn't understand just what was going on. I thought we were just having dinner. How gullible I was; I had no idea she was a lesbian!

When we went to the restaurant, Lily ordered angel hair spaghetti in a cream sauce for us both. After dinner we went back to my apartment and watched a video she'd brought along. It was just a story about a relationship between two women, not a porn film. The women became friends then lovers; it was very tastefully done with no graphic scenes, just implications.

You have to realize that when I'm psychotic, I can be led to believe just about anything. I was more than gullible, I was a donkey with a ring in my nose and a rope tied to it. Whoever grasped the rope could lead me anywhere. Lily was more than happy to do so.

As we sat on my sofa Lily laid on her back and pulled me close so I was on top of her, then we kissed. She was so tiny I don't think she even weighed 100 pounds. I rubbed my pelvis on her protruding right hip bone then instantaneously I discovered the sensation of an inner paradise: WOW!

I wasn't gay or bisexual, but being psychotic I would've had sex with the bed post or a door knob if it was attached to the floor. So why not a lesbian? Seth and I were separated; now Lily took his place.

I think Lily was looking for a mother figure. She was only 21 and I was 40. She bought me a book called *Lesbian Letters*, about women who discovered late in life that they were lesbians. Lily wanted a relationship with me and tried to convince me of that I was a lesbian. She sent me cards and letters containing words of love and affection.

Lily and I frequented bisexual bars that had a mixture of male and female couples. I cut my hair short to fit the bill of "dyke," a hateful word even then. One night when Lily and I were standing outside a gay bar, a man drove by in a car and screamed in a mean voice "Dykes!"

It made me feel very uneasy; was I that person they were screaming about? This began my questioning my sexual orientation, though I always liked men.

One night I went to the gay bar and sat on a barstool. An intoxicated young woman with blonde hair and blue eyes sat next to me. She wanted me to go home with her, just to cuddle, she said. I wasn't interested and didn't take her up on her proposal.

She was so intoxicated when she leaned toward me she fell off the stool onto the floor. I hope someone drove her home.

I was brought up Catholic and started to feel guilty about my behavior. I wasn't able to get the thought out of my mind that this was a mortal sin and I was heading to hell if I didn't change my behavior.

Seth came back into the picture and saved me from damnation. One night while playing pool at the gay bar he met Lily.

Lily said, "Susan, he is crazy."

I didn't disagree. I now had to choose between Lily and Seth. Even being psychotic I felt the relationship with Lily was a mortal sin. I felt there was no choice but to go back with Seth.

Of course Lily was quite upset. I told her she'd be the only lady in my life and there would never be another.

I'm not a lesbian but sometimes I wish I was. Lily told me that when two lesbians break up the emotional pain is more severe than that of heterosexuals. The two women will be on the same wavelength of emotional pain.

The one thing that came out of my relationship with Lily was that I could now see what men saw in women; the gentle touch and emotional support.

Now I have flashbacks. Thought it wasn't a good time in my life, it wasn't a bad time but somewhere in between.

A few years after our breakup I saw Lily's new girlfriend, Dottie. They lived in a single-family home with a pet ferret. Although Dottie was very nice, I was taken aback by her girlfriend, who was at least sixty.

Was Lily looking for a grandmother? I overheard Dottie tell Lily, "I'm about to retire, but you have a long life ahead of you and it's time for you to go."

These loving words were good advice.

PAUL, THE MILLIONAIRE

My sister Doris frequented Tucks, a small bar and grill. She struck up a conversation with Paul, a tall, slender man in his fifties with black curly hair and dark brown eyes. My sister described him as "a very kind individual having an awful lot of money."

In 1994 one million dollars was a lot of money. In addition he had a portfolio as thick as *Moby Dick.* Doris and Paul were just friends but my sister Doris had a plan with me in it. She asked, "Paul, would you like to meet my sister Susan?" His answer was yes.

One Saturday night, Doris arranged to get together at Tucks. We sat at a table for three. This important evening was the beginning of my friendship with Paul and our short-lived romance.

The following Saturday Paul invited me to dinner with his friends Barbara and Don, school teachers that Paul worked with for many years. Paul had retired at 50 with income from stocks he had acquired during his teaching years.

I can't believe what I said during dinner. We were at a really nice restaurant. I ordered shrimp and everyone else ordered surf and turf. I put my foot in my mouth before I'd even put my fork in. I blurted out, "Paul, will you marry me?"

I wasn't kidding. Being psychotic, whatever was on my mind came out of my mouth. I had no filter. I was serious about the marriage bit. I wanted to marry him and that was that. It didn't dawn on me that I barely knew this man.

He didn't say a thing but the look on his face said it all.

When I was leaving the restaurant, I somehow spilled the shrimp and butter onto my skirt and ruined it. Well, I guess I wouldn't get married that night.

Paul invited me to dinner one more time, just the two of us. In the middle of dinner he said in a subdued tone of voice, "I know you more in one evening than I know my friends of twenty years." I made quite an impression that evening. There was nothing to prevent the doorway of this mouth from shutting; all I could talk about was me, me and me.

Paul regretted that he didn't say yes to my proposal. He went on a rampage to win my affections and marry me. He bought me a brand-new car, a gold bracelet and a camcorder. Then he sent Doris and me on a Carnival cruise. Doris and I had a wonderful time and Paul paid the ticket. He didn't stop there—he bought Jack, the twins and me a trip to Disney Land, then gave us each $200 for spending money. With all these gifts I thought Santa Claus had come.

There were no strings attached as far as sex went; he was actually a virgin. *That's one problem I can fix*, I thought and I did… but only once. I had already experienced a marriage without love and I wasn't about to repeat that mistake to him or to me. I was out-of-control and I knew I would destroy Paul's life. Just because I was crazy didn't mean I'd lost my intelligence.

I said in a kind voice, "I don't love you. I can't marry you but we can stay friends."

Today we're still friends. Paul lives in an expensive condo in Rhode Island. I call him at least once a month to see how he is doing. Since 2000 he has had many medical problems, including seizures and four strokes. After Paul's last stroke I said in a firm voice, "I will come down and take care of you. Do you need me?"

Paul was quite certain he would be fine. People he knew were taking care of him properly. I was worried, though. I had to see for myself and went down to see him. I was pleasantly surprised that Paul truly was doing well. He is amazing. He still walks to breakfast every morning and has a full life, despite what he went through.

We recently had a discussion about the past and how crazy I was. He agreed with that statement and followed it with a hearty laugh. I asked, "Now aren't you glad you didn't marry me?" He started chuckling and said, "You bet."

He knew I was right on the money.

ALEX

When I was fifty I started frequenting a dance at the singles club in North Adams. I was the youngest one there; everyone else was over sixty. That's where I met Alex.

Alex was not like most men I had been dating; he wasn't looking for a real relationship or marriage. He was a kind person and let me know that marriage was out of the question. It just didn't work for him.

I really liked Alex; he actually had all his marbles. We would meet at the dance every Sunday night. He lived close by and when the dance was over, we went to his house for a drink or two of vodka, which he kept in the freezer.

Alex was quite good looking for his age. He had a slender build like that of a little boy. Our sex life was short-lived and so was the relationship—because of the night when I became psychotic.

The night the relationship ended was at a Halloween party. Most people there wore costumes and so did I. I wore a red deerskin Indian dress with moccasins and a medicine bag. I had silly feathers in my hair; I was a sight to see.

This was the night Alex told me our relationship was over. I tried my best to salvage it but he was stuck on "No."

Friday before the dance I had received a cortisone shot. By Sunday night I was psychotic.

All the signs and symptoms were there. I wore a fur coat from 1920, the warmest coat I've ever had. It was my grandmother's and had sentimental value. I remember this night so clearly; the tiger had burst its cage and it was destined for Alex. I flew into the dance like a witch on a broomstick, then asked Alex to dance and tried to seduce him. I became Virginia Woolf, a creature out of control.

When he denied my affections I returned to the table, flung my fur coat over my shoulders and stormed out the door like the wicked witch of the north. Everyone was watching me; I would never live this one down.

However, I didn't stop here—I was on the prowl. I stopped in a high-class bar and sat next to a man who obviously had no intentions of speaking to me. I could see this was a dead end, so left.

When I woke in the morning I knew something was wrong; desperately wrong. I was suicidal but I couldn't recognize the feelings. I knew enough to call the crisis team and drove to the emergency room at North Adams Regional Hospital. The therapist knew me well and I was admitted to Jones 2 at Berkshire Medical Center. When it was time for me to leave I called Alex and he gave me a ride home.

Now I'm the one that's over 65 at the dance. I go once or twice a year; Alex is still there. I used to talk nonstop when I was psychotic; why not? Now I just greet him and ask how he's doing; we have no real conversation. With my arthritis and sciatica I'm afraid my dancing days may be over. I am lucky I am walking. I'm no longer dancing like a crazy fool; a slow dance is more my style nowadays.

HEY, MRS. ROBINSON

I compare my manic personality to a butterfly flitting from one flower to the other. In some of my childhood pictures I have a Cheshire cat grin that I see even today in pictures taken when I am manic.

When I was even slightly manic that personality became apparent. I was a social butterfly then. I would become a tiger two decades later sexually encircling my target and I would say, "I am going to take you where you have never been before!" So I did.

I was getting high on the music and the atmosphere took me to a heightened level of awareness. I was experiencing low levels of mania. That is all I needed; I was about to fly!

This period in my life sex did not rule, but it was there lying dormant, waiting for the right time to surface.

I had problems with decision making and picking a lasting relationship. What makes this chapter important is that things were already starting to blossom in the way of a mental disorder. I had no idea that I was heading for disaster. I was already on the ups and downs of life's rollercoaster and ready and willing to take the ride. But unknown to me, I was out of control!

Even as I aged young people were attracted to me. I couldn't understand what they saw in little old me. I asked Barbara, my therapist, in an inquisitive voice, "I can't understand why young people find me alluring."

Barbara said with conviction, "Your chronological age will increase but you will never grow old to the outside world."

My manic personality was appealing; who could resist that?

My first encounter with a younger man was when I was 50. I was in a bikini, sunning myself in the backyard while a carpenter and his nephew Joe worked on my roof. At 26, Joe was a tall, handsome young man with brown hair and blue eyes and of course rippling with muscles.

In contrast his uncle Bob was 46, short and wiry. He was so strong he could lift heavy bundles of shingles on his shoulders then connect them to the roof with not a sigh of fatigue. It took my uncle and Joe days to complete the task.

I thought I would never see them again. But two days later I heard a knock at the door. I was surprised; I wasn't expecting anyone. Yet there, big as life, was Joe.

I said with a hearty voice, “Come in.”

He did and said, “Susan, come see the log cabin I built with my own two hands, a fine-looking camp that oversees Mt. Greylock.”

That invite sounded just fine with me. Since there was no such thing as GPS when I was fifty, I took down the directions. A dirt road led to a muddy driveway, the entrance to the camp. I was horrendous at following directions and this dirt road to the camp was scary—but the homeward trip was more than scary, more like *terrifying.*

I managed to find the camp. In the yard, there was a generator and a hand pump for water. Joe gave me the grand tour and it was quite impressive. The view was spectacular, just as he said it would be. It was early autumn and there was a chill in the air but when I opened the door and saw the potbelly wood stove, I knew it would keep us warm as toast.

Joe had other ways to keep me warm. He said, “Silly, sit on the chair while I stoke the fire.”

The chill began to leave the room as the stove heated it up. Joe walked slowly over to the couch where I sat.

My eyes almost popped out of their sockets; he had no shirt on and his jeans held no pocket, just a hole as big as a crescent moon. I had not seen this sight in 30 years and I didn’t say no to this opportunity.

Our romance lasted for six months but it was not romantic in any way; all we did was have sex. I remember Andrew telling me to use a condom, but I didn’t. And shouldn’t it have been the other way around, me telling Andrew to use a condom? I am lucky I never got a venereal disease.

Joe said with excitement, “Susan can I record this sex scene on my video camcorder?”

“Sure,” I said without thinking, stuck on *stupid* again.

When I told Jude she was furious and in an angry voice said, “Get that tape!”

But I didn’t. When I told my therapist she said softly, “Susan it’s sad that you do anything that men want; you can say NO.”

After that I did say no to sexual things I didn’t want to do. I ended the relationship with Joe after that.

As I was leaving his place it was raining pretty hard, so instead of taking the dirt road on the right I took the one on the left. After about 500 feet I saw some rocks; they were small at first then became big ones.

Oh, no; I was on the wrong road! I couldn't back up; I had to turn around. There was a little clearing; going in was no problem, but then I started backing up. My wheels spun. There was only a quarter tank of gas left and the night was more pitch black than I'd ever seen. It was still raining and I had no sleeping bag.

There would be no sleep for me. I was petrified. When daybreak came I walked down the stony wet path; it wasn't easy because I had open shoes. I saw many little camps on the side of the road but it was the end of the season so no one was living in them. I wanted to cry but I just kept walking.

Finally I saw a tiny shack on the left hand side of the dirt road. I knocked on the door and saw four young man getting ready for work. I explained my predicament and told them if they could drop me off at my home, I would pay them. They did.

I was to work that morning but that would be impossible, I was up all night. I called my boss and explained how I got stuck on a dirt road and was up all night and then I spilled the rest of the story.

He said, "Susan, if it was anyone else I would not believe them but since it's you I certainly do. Stay home and get some rest."

I've never gone down a dirt road again. When I told Joe what happened, he didn't even seem concerned.

I never went back to that camp again and it was about time to say goodbye anyway. "Mrs. Robinson" learned her lesson.

Or did she?

MRS. ROBINSON STRIKES AGAIN

"Mrs. Robinson" struck the second time when I returned from the Canary Islands, where I went even though I was having a psychotic break.

Two young men were sitting in my living room. My son Andrew had invited them for a week without even asking me.

The two were brothers; Joseph was 26 and Barry was 24. They were both very handsome young men with charming personalities. Joseph was tall, thin and had a devil-may-care attitude, while Barry was shy and didn't say very much.

I had two photo albums; one was a family album and the other was from the Canary Islands. Somehow they got mixed up and Joseph saw a photograph of me getting out of the pool topless with a string for the bottom. I had a great body for 50 and my face wasn't too bad either. I'm not bragging; it's just the truth.

The next morning I was up early, sitting on the sofa with a cup of coffee. Before I knew it Joseph was sitting beside me.

He whispered softly in my ear, "Can I kiss you?"

All I could think of was *I haven't brushed my teeth yet.*

But I replied, "Sure, why not."

When I was psychotic I did things I normally would not do in my sane mind. Everyone was sleeping so we tiptoed up to my bedroom.

I undressed and he said, "Wow you're beautiful."

He proceeded to drop his drawers and his shirt went flying. I said to myself, *Is this really happening? God, he is gorgeous.*

My mind was stuck on go; psychosis is an animal and now Joseph was my prey. The next morning he knocked on my bedroom door, ready for round two. I tried to keep from my sons that I was sleeping with their friend.

When Joseph and Barry headed for their home in South Carolina I never expected to hear from Joseph again.

Wrong again, Susan. Joseph called frequently. After a while Andrew became suspicious; Joseph talked to me longer than he did to Andrew. Yet knowing my son he thought, *Who would sleep with that old bag?* and he never put two and two together.

Eventually Joseph suggested that I come to his home when his parents were on vacation. There was no way this gal was driving to South Carolina. I declined his invitation but that didn't stop him from calling. I finally discouraged him and the calls stopped.

A bit of clarity must have poked through so I could make an intelligent decision to stop. When I look back I had no shame. I actually told Andrew what happened. My reasoning was I worried if I died Joseph could throw in Andrew's face: "I slept with your mother."

Now Andrew could say, "I know; mom already told me."

It's hard to believe a mother could act like this but under the grip of psychosis, anything was possible.

You might say my whole life was a big blunder. I was always in the moment, never thinking of the consequences of my actions; this kind of thinking got me into a lot of trouble. But I also had quite the adventures

I started spending money and calling Europe: yes, Adam and Hans. I must say I was quite the fool. I invited them to Mexico and paid for Adam's ticket.

None of this materialized and I was stuck with Adam's ticket. I put on quite a show at the airlines to get a refund. I told them he died in a motorcycle accident in Austria.

They wanted a death certificate. I said, "I tried with no luck."

With the technology today I certainly would not get away with this one. They finely conceded and refunded my ticket.

I learned a few phrases in German and one was, "I love you."

Finally, the romance fizzled out. He was halfway around the world. What did I expect? I was irrational of course and thought that this could happen but as time passed my intellect said no way!

I was spending all kinds of money. This was a definite sign that I was not quite stable. I thought that this was going to be the last hoorah.

Of course Jude heard about this. I think she wanted to shock some sense into me, but not in this state of mind. I was driven by a force so strong no one could intervene. Stability was so far away, years in the making and included dealing with

DANCE DANGER—BONES

1996 was the first time Mark and I took a trip to Cancun, Mexico. Unbeknownst to me this could have been my last. We attended a bar named Bones. It was packed and we snatched up the two empty seats at the bar right away.

When we ordered our drinks the bartender put them on the top of his head. He crouched down so we could remove the drink from his head; that's how he served us. There was a big jar full of tips and I can see why; they never spilled a drop.

The dance floor was full; the band played typical wild Mexican music. I wanted to dance but the floor was too crowded. I needed an empty floor with enough room to whirl around like the Tasmanian devil.

To use the ladies' room I had to go past the dance floor and up a huge set of stairs to the right. To my surprise, when I went back to the bar the dance floor was empty.

Because of the intense mania I was experiencing that night my mind was dancing at a fast pace and the wild music only made it more evident. The music was like a mating call and this bird flew using the end of her skirt as wings flapping in the air. I danced as gracefully as a figure skater on ice. When the music stopped I walked slowly back to the bar and sat down. The bartender placed a shot of in front of me. He said, "*İMagnífico!*"

Mark turned his head to me and shrieked, "Didn't you hear you had a standing ovation?"

I replied, "I didn't hear a thing."

I was in my world, my inward universe where no one else was invited. I used this technique for many years to keep the demons at bay.

Mark drank the shot of tequila and whispered in my ear, "Susan, take off your underwear and put it in the shot glass."

I didn't hesitate. I pulled up my skirt, making sure my underwear was clean before placing it in the glass. There were many people around me who could have called the police. But I had no fear; the music enhanced my mania, leaving no fear of the consequences to my actions.

Mark grabbed my arm and said, "Let's go."

We ran out the front door and caught a cab waiting at the door. I wonder what the bartender did with my underwear. Maybe it's still there, placed in a frame above the bar.

When I was 19 and living on my own my sister and I frequented the bars Friday and Saturday nights. Doris and I had conversations consisting of our opinions about the women at the bar, like how old they were and how we had it all over them as we were so young. In actuality they had it all over us. These women had life experience with dangerous situations, especially concerning men.

One time I got into a very dangerous situation. How I got myself into the circumstances I did is a bit vague. I only remember being invited into a car by a very soft spoken man who said, "Let's go to my car. People will not overhear the conversation; it's more private there."

That summer night I was wearing a white short-sleeved dress with daisies printed on it. I was "stuck on stupid." I didn't realize the danger I was subjecting myself to.

He told me he was a principal at a nearby elementary school; I asked myself, *How dangerous can this be? The principal of the school.*

I didn't even know his name. He was an authority figure; fear wasn't present because of his stature in the community. Oh boy, was I wrong.

As soon as I entered the car he was all over me. How did I get myself into this? I was immature, naïve and out of touch with reality concerning these situations.

He didn't rape me but circled his legs around mine and began to hump my leg like a dog in heat. I pleaded with him to stop but either he didn't hear me or he did hear me but didn't stop. This seemed familiar; he was an authority figure like the doctor of my youth, though my memories of him and his heinous crimes against me had not surfaced yet.

When the man finished his final hump he let go, saying sternly, like scolding a student, "Whatever you do don't tell anyone."

Doris was still in the bar and had no idea what was happening to me. I felt embarrassed when I told her. She said, "Let's get out of this dive."

We grabbed our pocketbooks and never went back to this bar again.

Doris wondered in a confused voice, "Why is it men age eight to eighty find you so attractive? It isn't just this case; it's all the time. What is that you have that I don't?"

I replied, "I don't know."

That I wasn't ugly was a plus. A few decades later we would understand it was my manic personality. What Doris didn't possess was mental illness. That was nothing to be jealous of.

Late one night I entered the dance hall with my boyfriend. Why can't I remember, why is it so vague? It's almost like a dream yet truly happened. I was doing my usual, dancing by myself. I didn't see it but my boyfriend did; men made a circle around me. I can see why. My dancing was very seductive and everywhere I danced, every man in the place had his eyes on me. But this was different. This time I was the prey, not them.

I was rescued by my boyfriend, who took my arm and pulled me through the circle of onlookers.

This could have been a dangerous situation. In my era gang-bang situations existed, in movies where women were held down on pool tables and raped by a small mob of men. In those days they got away with it. Most of the women were too ashamed to report it to the authorities. I had no fear; this incident did not stop me from dancing just the way I want to.

Once, I read in the paper that they were hiring belly dancers at a bar in downtown Providence, Rhode Island. The pay was so great I had to try out. I said to myself, *I can do anything, especially dancing. I will check on it right away.*

It was about nine o'clock the night I strolled into the bar to meet with the manager.

I asked, "Is the job taken yet?"

He said "No" and went to the back room.

While there a man sitting to my right invited me to his car. Common sense went out the window and I went.

But this time I was lucky; this man was there to help me. His car was spectacular; if it had wings I bet it could fly.

The man told me he was a gangster. I wasn't scared; I wanted to see him again. *(Hello! What's wrong with this picture?)* But even though he was a gangster, he had a heart and discouraged me from pursuing this employment. He told me the job was not what I thought it was; it was more than dancing.

"Someone as agreeable as you need not get involved with such a place. I think a waitress job, but not here," he said.

The gangster wanted to save me from all the riffraff that entered this place. If it wasn't for him I wouldn't be reading the employment section, I'd be reading my obituary!

A few years passed and I was working at Roger Williams's Hospital. In order to stay stable and keep my mania at a low level, sun and exercise were important to achieve. I was a beach bum and a dancing fool. I went dancing two times a week at a local bar, always alone; other women cramp my style.

The dress I wore that night was silky and fit like a glove. I was enjoying sitting at the bar drinking, listening to everybody's conversations and, of course, dancing. One man there who I had seen more than once came up to me and asked in a puzzled voice, "You're a prostitute?"

I said, "Of course not. Why would you think this?"

He replied, "The way you dress, you're so friendly and you're alone."

"I'm sorry to disappoint you, sir. You have me all wrong. This is just what I am; a friendly woman, young and beautiful, but not a prostitute."

One night one of the patrons I was dancing with invited me to his hotel room. I never slept with him; I told him I had my period. I did this more than once to get out of sleeping with men.

The oddest thing occurred when I stayed with these men. I could never fall asleep; it was too intimate for me. I always left before sunrise. (Would I turn to dust? Was I a vampire in a past life?)

This particular man woke before I left and handed me golden cufflinks engraved with a scorpion, his sign of the zodiac and also mine. It wasn't payment; it was a kind gesture. I find it unusual that the cufflinks stand out in my mind more than the man himself. He is only a blur, not even a shadow in my mind.

Decades later this would be the opposite. The vampire lust in my eyes paralyzed my victims, bringing them to a place inside themselves that they never knew existed or felt before. They became the walking dead without me. My fangs reached into their very souls. It was as though I had branded them with a permanent scar, causing them to perpetually seek the eyes with no bottom.

"SON"DAYS

When Andrew, Michael and Jack were living with me, my house became hostile and combative. Michael and Jack had physical fights ending in massive hemorrhaging, blood, cuts, bumps and bruises, on one or both of them.

I am only skimming the surface with all the goings-on in this house; this is just another book inside the book of my life.

My three sons lived with me as adults; they punched holes in walls and kicked out windows. Two sons were aggressive and the other was passive.

Michael and Jack almost killed one another and this was no exaggeration; it was painful to watch. It was like Cain and Abel, but I wasn't going to let this happen.

Writing the book at this time brings back so many memories of Jack and Michael, fighting in mortal combat. Did this actually happen? Yes, undeniably so! It was another hell.

When Michael and Andrew were years old they visited me in North Adams for a two-week vacation. Seth was still in the picture. I have a photograph of Michael, Andrew and Seth holding each other's hands, running and jumping into the pool. As I recall it was a funny photograph.

I was back to work at Willowood. I'm not quite sure how long I had been working; possibly two years. Even after two years, working was difficult.

I took the boys to a couple of places; one was an old mill where artists came to use the monoprint printing press, which measured 7'4 x 3'4. There was an exhibit, all of six-foot monoprints, that the boys and I attended and one captured my attention. It was a six-foot vampire monoprint with wings of an angel, snow white hair and a candelabra at the base.

I was truly captivated by the painting of a face a young artist was working on. It resembled someone in extreme agony and it caught my eye. I related to his torment. I had to have this painting and bought it.

The figure was at least six feet tall. I asked the artist what he was thinking about when he did this. He replied, "A Greek God that thought his children were going to kill him. He devoured his children at birth, all except one, and she did kill him."

A not-so-obvious figure was in the abdomen; it looked like a fetus. I still have this painting framed and I'm looking at it right now.

The boys and I were having a great time. This was good stress but it doesn't matter if it's good or bad stress; stress is stress and it finally became overwhelming.

After a week the twins had to go back. Their father was not happy with this but I realized I needed a week to recover in order to go back to work. Stress is an issue you can't ignore; at this time I was still walking the balancing beam. I could fall at any time.

Work, which was a major stress factor, had to come first and there was no way to eliminate it. I had to simplify my life and keep as much stress out as imaginable.

I was still having problems with sleep; Lithium was the main cause. Thirst was its main side effect. Every hour I would wake, drink a full glass of orange juice, go back to sleep and in another hour I had to empty my bladder then back to sleep, all night long. This went on for three years with no REM sleep.

Eugene was in prison for a crime he didn't commit, adding another living hell, fifteen long years of waiting for his release.

This I could not bear. Inside me flesh-eating, shark-like teeth ripped. As they reached the surfaces between the sternum and rib cage where my heart lay, they managed to shred it bit by bit. My heart was nonexistent, not a beat left and no blood left for tears. I opened my mouth to scream but not a sound came out.

Eugene was charged with a crime he refused to plead guilty to. He could have pled guilty and taken a plea bargain, then received three to five years. Eugene was telling the truth and thought God would save him.

They found him guilty and gave him fifteen years. In Bridgewater State Hospital he was diagnosed with Bipolar Disorder and put on medication.

Life was a living hell for him. He was 26 and unaware of the danger of prison life. Determined, he went into the population; courage was his motivator. Now he says it was stupid to do that. His decision made his illness worse and when he was released it crippled him.

While he was there he never told me the horror stories that transpired. He postponed these frightening tales until he was out. Now he just lives in a bigger cell, the unforgiving world.

If I were able to convey the true facts to you, you surely would believe me, or have a definite doubt. He is innocent! He wishes he was guilty. Then he would've took the three to five and saved his youthful years and most of all, his sanity.

Unashamed, Eugene said, "Mom, I could accept this punishment if I did what I was accused of."

His public defender betrayed him; Eugene was set up.

At the first trial my illness was present. I was without a job or savings. The hearing before the trial bail was $2,000.00. I needed the bail money to hire a lawyer for my divorce.

Three years before his release, after working hard for fifteen years saving money, I had the ability to pay the ideal lawyer.

Now I was balanced, not that sick person I used to be. There would be no betrayal. Money talks.

I recall my optimism praying on my knees near the toilet in the lady's room. My prayers were answered; YES!

The stress caused my mental illness to be pushed to the maximum test. Hunched over, wrapping my arms around the toilet, I heaved uncontrollably, feeling like my innards lay in the bowl.

"Judge, please release Eugene into my custody," I asked tearfully.

"Yes," he replied.

When he was released, two women officers met me at Friendly's in Greenfield. We pulled into the parking lot at the same time. I couldn't believe this was real but it was.

Eugene wore an old tattered, faded white t-shirt, green prison pants and boat sneakers with no support, all tattered and worn. He bent slightly, gave me a hug and shakily started to cry, whimpering.

My son! This took place seven years ago. The memory is embedded in my soul.

Eugene has been home now seven years. He's like my private comedian. He makes me laugh so hard I cry. I could write a book on his experiences. All I can say is thank god he never told me what went on in the penal institution until he came home. He suffers still from being imprisoned for a crime he never committed.

When Michael was eight years old, he was quite thrilled because he found almost every piece of jewelry I lost. I recall the time he pulled out a wallet full of cash from behind some insulation in the basement. "I am a good finder," he would say.

"You sure are, Michael," I would agree.

Ten years later, he would say, "You never count your money, enabling me to steal it right under your nose."

Even today I don't count it, but now I use a credit card to stop his abuse. Michael stole; if it wasn't nailed to the floor, it was gone.

I attributed this to his life of drug usage with an untreated mental illness, spinning him like a tornado. "Tornado" was Michael's nickname; sometimes he was called "The Hurricane." That was the level of energy he possessed, with a wrecking ball close behind him.

When Michael and Jack had their first fight, Michael took a copper pot to Jack's head and blood sprayed everywhere, covering curtains and wallpaper. Their faces were drenched with blood. The force truly dented the copper pot!

One time Michael and Jack started to fight in Jack's bedroom. I tried to stop them; not a good idea as the television went soaring by my face. Michael took his foot and started to smash the side of Jack's head. Michael could've snapped his neck, but instead Jack's ear was dangling, blood everywhere; it needed to be reattached with many stitches, what a mess!

Michael started to retreat down the stairs to the front door because Jack was loose now and after him. Michael tripped over the cord to the vacuum cleaner and Jack gave it a tug. It wrapped around Michael's foot and Jack was reeling him in like a fish he had snagged.

Michael was trying to break free; you could hear his nails scratching, grinding into the floor, as he tried to hold his place. Then he got loose and bolted out the front door screaming, "It's over, it's over!"

Jack was at Michael's heels, but Michael had a head start and Jack lost the race. Of course this was not the last of it.

Later, Michael grabbed Jack by the throat and Jack hit Michael in the head with a frying pan. This time Michael required numerous stitches. Thank God there was no permanent damage; Jack could've killed him.

This is the story of two brothers in chaos, with an out-of-control mental illness. They didn't take medication for their illnesses, just street drugs. Their mental illness played a big part in their destructive behavior and the drug abuse in their early to mid- twenties.

Soon after my sons came to live with me, they began to take turns being admitted to psychiatric units. Michael was the first to be admitted to Jones 2, the psychiatric unit on Berkshire Medical Center. Jones 3 was a psychiatric unit for more violent behavior.

Michael and Andrew took their turns on Jones 3, but because of dangerous actions towards themselves, not to each other. Jack and Michael harmed one another; Andrew never physically attacked his brothers.

Jack spent the least amount of time on the psych wards, while Michael holds the record, of at least 35 times and that is just a guesstimate.

One time when Michael was eighteen, I took him to the emergency room. He was so out-of-control he was kicking the dashboard with his feet and yelling, "I am going to kill you!"

When I stopped the car to let him out, Michael took a matte knife and cut into his palm until it was soaked with blood, causing extensive damage. He smeared his hand dripping of blood on the leather seat of the car then grabbed the door and tried to snap it off at the hinges.

I proceeded forward until Michael became unfastened, then he dashed like a sprinter, destination: the emergency room entrance.

"You slut," he yelled as loud as he could.

He hurled a rock at me. Since he was young and strong it had the velocity of a speeding bullet as it slid across the top of the car and onto the ground.
Sadly, this was normal behavior for Michael. There were many times he yelled and kicked and threatened to kill me; his face and body revealed fury.

He displayed his rage as a passenger in my car many times. Serenity and calmness were not his forte. He would steal anything that wasn't nailed down, then sell it to support the drug usage that consumed his every waking moment. You would think by that time I'd be frightened. No, not me! I dismissed it because I related to their illness and held myself responsible for passing on the gene of MADNESS!

Since then some time has passed and Michael has regret and shame. If anyone mentions his past addictions, even in a humorous way, it upsets him and he doesn't want to hear it; sometimes he tries to defend himself. Now, knowing this, we all avoid speaking about his addictive behavior and his previous actions to the family.

I found a paper Michael wrote once describing what he thought about himself as an addict, at 17 years old. In his own words:

Negative by Michael

Emotional anxiety causes more paranoia; ultimately causing depression; which destroys one's motivational drive. Drug use in a severe manner causes extreme psychological damage. This causes lack of self-esteem. This makes my life hard to manage; in any function. While heavily using the only thought in my mind is to get high. No remorse is given to anything. I'm so unsure of myself and what I must accomplish. The pressure is multiplied by 100 times the normal person's amount. I am so, so fucking scared! I know what I must do while trying to undo my addictive way. The way I've treated my family and friends makes me feel ashamed, guilty and total remorse; for what I put them through. I feel cursed!

My sons' father was never any help at all. He would post bail for Michael, but emotional support was not there for me or for the children. If I had to count how many times they were in jail and hospital psych wards, I don't think anyone would believe me. It was like a part time job with no pay. Was this the 1800s, with Susan as slave to her sons?

Sad to report, Michael fell back into his addictive patterns. He moved into a drug infested area; that didn't help matters. One of the reasons he gave was the rent was low, something he could afford.

"Drugs are everywhere," was his excuse.

I replied, "If you're an alcoholic you don't spend all your time hanging around bars because eventually you will have a drink and you're right back where you were before."

For the last thirteen years their father showed no interest in them other than sending money, money being a death sentence, money for more drugs. Michael, Jack and Andrew needed a father, not a dollar!

I called Isaac. "Get Michael out of that cesspool," I said in a stern voice. He was in denial about the long sleeves Michael wore even in the summer to cover his track marks.

I left many messages on his phone. He never would talk to me, even about the children; I knew them better than he did.

Finally Isaac listened to me and took Michael under his wing. I feared if he didn't Michael would not survive because the latest drug of choice would surely take his life! I do believe in God and God answered my prayers and removed him from the unhealthy situation; my son would live!

His father made the best choice and seized the opportunity to act before it was too late. Thank you to the father of my children, taking on this moral fight without hesitation and in doing so saving Michael's life.

Michael and his dad help each other now. Before we were married Isaac said he wanted children in his old age. Mental illness and drug abuse have made it financially impossible for Jack and Michael to help him; they're both on disability.

Jack and Michael are adults and respectful, no longer the crazy kids I used to know.

Michael and Andrew are twins. Andrew had more qualities of his dad than the other boys.

Andrew and Michael were healthy babies but contracted whooping cough at the age of three months. Andrew almost died but Michael wasn't even hospitalized.

Thank God for the intern at Massachusetts General Hospital who diagnosed him! He asked if anyone had said anything about *pertussis,* another word for whooping cough. None of the doctors at New Wellesley Hospital had any idea what was happening. Andrew wasn't eating and was withering away.

"Rest assured, there is no problem, give him some honey," the doctor said.

I gave Andrew honey and he stopped breathing.

I screamed, "Isaac, Andrew is not breathing!"

Isaac came in like a flash and resuscitated him, then he was fine. What a scary moment that was; I thought I would lose him. Now on the back of the honey jar it warns not to give honey to infants.

I said sternly, "Get him to Mass General."

Andrew was in isolation for quite a long time. Of course he got excellent care and was able to come home. Their pediatrician said, "We just had another case of whooping cough, also with twins. They died."

Oh, how lucky I felt! But it wasn't just luck that saved my son. I was persistent, telling the doctors I never heard a cough like this.

Sally, Isaac's sister, had lost one twin when he choked on a piece of apple. I thought I might lose mine but didn't. Thank God! Michael and Andrew had a tough journey but they made it.

It took a while to make Jack, Michael and Andrew accountable for their actions and to let go of the guilt I felt for passing down the gene of madness. They were lucky, though; they had Bipolar 2, unlike me, with Bipolar 1; a more sinister affliction, never to go away.

When Jack came to live with me at age twenty, all hell broke loose. He would put his face close to mine and scream threats, I thought he might carry them out but he never did. But my house was no longer my own. Jack ruled the roost; he was intimidating, to say the least.

He used to say to Michael and Andrew, "I can get into mom's head, so you better watch it."

What he meant was he could persuade me into his way of thinking so he could get his way. It became apparent that *I* should leave my house; they weren't budging.

Jack had his turn in the emergency room. He swallowed a bottle of anti-psychotic meds and mixed it with alcohol. His gait was slowed and his speech was slurred. He should have been admitted. He went by cab to the hospital; he knew where he belonged, the psychiatric unit. Wasn't it evident he was attempting to take his life? Yet they let him go.

When Jack and Michael were in the slammer they took turns tormenting the police, giving them a merciless verbal attack. They double-teamed the police and drove them nuts. If the cops were interrogating someone in Jack's presence he would yell, "Don't say a word."

Jack was well versed in what you should and shouldn't say.

Michael and Jack were in trouble a lot and spent many days in court putting up bail money. It got so the judge and I knew each other by name.

The judge was merciful, partly because mental illness was involved and explained their actions. I'm not saying they shouldn't have been responsible for their actions but the judge took their illness into consideration.

Often five o'clock in the morning was the time to take one of my sons to the hospital. It could be any day, time, or situation. This messed with my sleep big time and didn't help my illness; mania was guaranteed. This went on for quite a few years.

Finally, I was unable to take it any longer and said, with conviction in my voice, "There will be no more posting bail. It's over. No more court appearances either."

I succeeded in not going totally and completely off my rocker. This was just the beginning of ten years of never-ending chaos with my sons, just a minuscule insight into the absurdity of ***my life!***

Never under any circumstances provoke a fight with a person like Jack when he's crazed. The energy and strength he possesses is endless and he doesn't know when to stop. When Jack was 14 he had confrontations with a boy named Sol about a girl Jack had impregnated.

Sol surprised Jack, rendering him defenseless. He sucker punched him and Jack hit the pavement, face down. Jack's only defense was his mouth; he bit a hole in Sol's ear but didn't bite it off. After all, Jack wasn't Michael Tyson, heavyweight champ, but his reaction was close. Sol shrieked, losing his grip. In a millisecond, Jack sprang into action and used his soccer skills, kicking him so hard he broke three ribs and Sol had to be hospitalized

American Indians believed evil spirits consume crazy people and they steered clear of them. It's hard to discern where all that negative energy comes from, but Jack had the strength of four men. I don't think it's a chemical imbalance or testosterone. It's like someone or something takes over; exactly what, I don't know.

I remember when Jack entered kindergarten. The first day I was called. The teacher was hysterical and said, "The janitor is unable to release Jack from holding onto a table leg. Jack won't let go!"

By the time I got there Jack released his hand.

After this incident things seemed to calm down. Then when Jack was about ten years old he turned over his desk. He was unable to control himself; he was so fidgety and couldn't sit still for long periods of time.

Every three hours Jack could get timeout. He would go into the playground and shoot hoops for about twenty minutes. The doctor thought he had Attention Deficit Disorder.

Jack always wants to be number one—I can relate to that! Attention Deficit Disorder mimics Bipolar disorder and the only difference between them is while one may want to be number one and rule the roost, the other may also have a mental illness.

When Jack was 12 he was a guard on the basketball team. He was known for his three-point-shots and he was everywhere. That year he received a trophy for the most valuable player though he was the shortest guy on the team.

Isaac and I were in the throes of a divorce at the time. While we sat in the bleachers I commented "Isaac, Jack has Bipolar Disorder. Look at him; he's everywhere. He radiates energy."

Isaac replied in a mean voice, "You're no psychiatrist."

I didn't reply but I was thinking to myself, *I don't have to be a psychiatrist I see myself in him.*

Jack played in almost every sport. He pitched a no-hitter and his soccer skills were exceptional. The older he became, the more apparent his mental illness became. Scholastics seemed more difficult, especially reading; he even has this problem now but it's getting better.

Jack's father was in denial even though Jack's behavior deteriorated as far as society was concerned. It would take Isaac decades to admit Jack was sick with (BPD).

While all the craziness with my sons was going on, I was still working forty hours a week. I didn't realize they were taking drugs and that makes me look like a fool. They all called me "MENTAL MOM."

It didn't bother me because it was the truth. I had just suffered a psychotic break and was about to lose my job. It didn't help when Michael called me at work one day. "Mom, they're raiding the house, they're pulling everything apart!"

Hearing this, slumped in a chair, I almost dropped the phone, not believing what was spoken. Why would police officers want to raid my house? I was crying now.

"Go home," one of my coworkers said.

Being good in a crisis was a skill I possessed, but this one took me by surprise. I needed help and I called the crisis team. I was losing it and asked, "What should I do?"

The crisis clinician replied, "Do nothing."

What a great concept; *do nothing!* Those words put me back together. When I reached the house there were three police cars, a tan Cadillac and a cruiser. This is the first time I had police at my house, but it would not be the last; as a matter of fact it became an everyday occurrence. If there wasn't a police car there would be an ambulance. For ten years my house became a hospital and police station. Jack was sitting on the front porch and leaning on a case of beer. He held a can of beer in his hand and sipped it while he laughed, taunting and provoking the detective. Jack was being disrespectful to all five of the officials. It seemed like he was having a hell of a time and he knew just how far he could push them without being arrested.

The police refused to let me into my house. It was chilly out and the head honcho let me sit in his cruiser. Even though I struggled not to, the stress freed me to babble like an idiot. The police believed my sons were selling drugs. It never crossed my mind that they were taking drugs. The detective handed me a search warrant. "Are you Marie Rose?" he asked.

"No, my name is Susan Rose," I said.

Four hours passed before they let us back into the house. We were told to sit on the couch and stay put. They ripped the house apart, flipping over mattresses, looking in drawers and the attic. There was $1,500.00 in an envelope to purchase a car for Jack that very day. Though it was mine it was confiscated as drug money and I never got it back. $80 was also mine, in plain sight; they took that too. I also had a couple of thousand dollars in my pocketbook that day, not unusual and it was open. According to the law an open pocketbook could be searched. An officer who knew me whispered, "Close your bag."

If my pocketbook was closed, no rummaging or seizure of its contents was allowed. What a nice guy. He knew Susan Rose was no drug dealer.

"Don't say anything, mom," Jack said to me as they raided my house. What was he talking about? I asked, "What should not be said? I have nothing to hide."

"Didn't you know your children are taking drugs?" one of the police officers asked.

My answer was "No."

Andrew was never in jail but he was no saint. When he saw the attention his brothers were getting for hostile, negative behavior, he slammed the door and ran in a fast clip to the old shed in the backyard, then knocked out a board. "I want attention too!"

"What are you doing?" I shrieked.

"It looks like negative feedback gets your attention, Mom."

"What the hell!" I yelled.

"When the baby birds start shitting in the nest, mother bird gives them a push out!" my therapist said.

It took ten years to give them the shove. Fly or perish, that's what I say.

I gave ten years of my life to help them. Michael and Andrew are now 32. Michael is clean, no drugs, living with Isaac. They have their problems like all of us but the chaos is no longer there. I am no longer their taxi cab.

Now Jack and Michael live peacefully but it took quite a while. Now they take their medication and act like real brothers.

HEY, JUDE

Jude and I met at Saint Elisabeth Hospital in Brighton, Massachusetts. We were both respiratory therapists. I was 26 and taught her how to perform pulmonary function testing, which shows the severity of lung functions. Most of our patients had chronic obstructive lung disease. Jude was a quick learner and easily picked up the calculations to interpret lung functions. We worked well together; our friendship flourished and lasted for thirty years.

A doctor, Jude and I did pulmonary function studies on pregnant women. We did an excellent job. We published a paper: "'New Lung Functions and Pregnancy.' February 1, 1977; from the St. Elizabeth Hospital Boston and Tuffs University School of Medicine; published in American Journal of Obstetrics and Gynecology." The doctors thanked Jude and me for our valuable assistance. I was in my early twenties and never had my name in print; this was very special. It gave me confidence and made me feel like I was worth something.

My husband at the time made me feel the exact opposite: stupid and worthless.

Isaac was dead set against my relationship with Jude. He was sure that she had influence over me. This was true but only to some extent. I used her as a sounding board. After I vented I would say, "Isaac is getting better." Even though he wasn't.

This marriage would last fourteen years and end in a disgusting, vicious manner in 1989. Now with Isaac out of the way the next twelve years were ours. That's when we started to travel. The first destination was Cancun, Mexico.

This was a thirteen hour plane ride. When we reached the hotel I said, "Let's go to the casino. It's only a mile away."

I'd learned this information from the lady at the front desk and was about to put a plan into action. Jude would have nothing to do with this. She was tired. It was a thirteen hour plane ride. But I wasn't tired, not with mania as my fuel! I was ready and willing to go, about to light up the place with my heightened awareness.

Jude asked, "Are you crazy?"

The answer was yes. Here I was in another country, stepping into the darkness, all alone, with no fear. The cab arrived at midnight and drove me there. Like the old saying goes, "Hold on to your hat, you're on the ride of your life.

I've been to casinos in the United States but this casino was a closet compared to the ones in the U.S. It seemed right; this was just a small island.

I was wearing a black, sequined gown with spaghetti straps; I had a beautiful tan. I looked stunning as I entered the casino through two large glass doors. I stopped at the front desk, showed my identification, then took the elevator to the second floor and sat at the blackjack table with an air of arrogance.

This was my game. I hardly ever lost. I wasn't a card counter; I was just lucky. I sat on the power seat, the first seat to the right, facing the dealer. At twelve o'clock, midnight, the bewitching hour, a tall slender good-looking man with an olive complexion started a conversation with me. His name was Hans, he was Austrian and had an accent. His friend Adam knew only a few words in English. Hans became our translator.

Hans said his friend Adam, who was sitting to my left, thought that I was the sexiest women he had ever seen.

He was right about the sexiest women part; he wouldn't meet another like me. I was a crazed love goddess roaming the earth, more like prowling, ready to pounce on her unexpected pray. Adam became my delicious meal.

Adam swung my seat around. It was hard not to stare; there was something behind his eyes I dared not see. His eyes were like mirrors and I only saw my own reflection…as if I were a reverse vampire. We were face-to-face now and he said, "Ooh là là!"

Hans said Adam wanted to take me out for a drink.

I said, "No, but let's all go dancing tomorrow night."

That wasn't the last thing I said. Within seconds I said in an enthusiastic voice, "Here is my hotel and room number. Tonight we can dance all night; I have no plans."

Was I insane giving them my room number and my hotel? They could have been serial killers or slave runners and Jude and I their victims.

We danced all night. Then Hans and Adam escorted me to the front door of my hotel room and said, "Ciao."

In Italian, this means goodbye, but we would soon become inseparable. We would need no translations. We were wrapped in duct tape so, so, close you could say we were crazy glued together, emphasis on crazy!

I can't identify with this person today. After many years of counseling, my therapist said in a steady voice, "Susan, someday this life of madness will feel as though it never existed." She was right.

I will never forget madness running riot, driving me over the limits, from madness to insanity; wild nights and crazy days intertwining mind, spirit and body with Adam.

I told Jude about my adventure and she was horrified, but that didn't stop me. Hans, Adam and I went dancing the following evening. Adam was a great dancer. As we were dancing, unbeknownst by me, I was in his arms. We danced like this until the music stopped. I thought, *How intense and romantic is this?*

We went to another night spot that had music with a rhythmic quality resembling Native American drums. I danced to the beat as my ancestral native blood drove through my veins. Hans started to dance with me. I could see that he was fascinated with me; this could be dangerous. If Adam saw, he would be furious, even though they were friends.

When they went back to the bar, Adam and Hans had words. Adam seemed annoyed with Hans. I heard Adam say, "She is my girl!" They talked a bit and everything went back to normal. That was the end of their discussion

Before we left the bartender played an interesting tune, hitting a bottle on the bar with a spoon. An old woman approached me and in broken English she said, "I loving you're dancing" and kissed me on the cheek.

Adam was holding on real tight and was not about to let go, that was for damn sure. He knew there was something special in those eyes of mine that had no bottom, but what? He would soon discover what stimulated and fascinated him. He would think, Wow, this woman is receptive to anything. *(Is she the devil in a blue dress, blue dress on, devil with the blue dress on?)*

Jude didn't come dancing that night, but that didn't last long. Adam's friend Hans was persuasive. She was at least ten years older than him. I don't think he even recognized this. She would never admit it, but she had the time of her life. They invited us to dinner and cooked a delicious meal, then we drank red wine. I have a sweet photo of Hans and Jude embracing each other as they kissed.

She was not completely receptive to Hans's desires. After that, the romance started to dwindle. She was a great kisser and said that was the thing she liked the best, but that's about as far as it went. Hans was disappointed but what could he do? This was her nature.

One time Jude and I met Hans' and Adam's friends and went to the casino. Their friend had an argument with one of the dealers and made a big scene. I never saw someone so infuriated. But in the end he got his way and his money was returned; everything went back to usual. After the incident we all crammed into a cab and headed for our hotels. That was to be our last venture to the casino.

She gave good advice, but I hardly ever took it. It wasn't that I didn't know better; I couldn't help myself. I had no conception of what was moral concerning Susan. At this stage of the game anything was on the docket: no shame, emotion, fear or consequences of my actions. She would shudder at the things I did; you could say we were the odd couple when it came to sex.

I have a photograph of Adam and Jude. He picked her up in his arms and swung her around over his head. You should see the horror on Jude's face. She was with his friend Hans that night and didn't expect to be hurled through the air by Adam. Adam was a bit crazy in this area, showing his masculinity in a physical nature, but Jude didn't want any part in this. She wasn't the crazy one there; neither was Hans.

Adam said, "Susan, please accompany me to Bangkok after this trip."

Thank God I had one brain cell left. He was a world traveler. Saying yes would have been a disaster. If not for Jude, there would be a horror story and I would not be the one to tell it. I was on the biggest high of my life. I am sure I would have gone, that's for damn sure; you could place a bet and it would be a hundred present in your favor.

One night after making love, Adam said, "I've never had such good sex in all of my life."

After that my name became "Love Baby." He would beat his fist to his chest shouting, "I loving you, love baby!"

His chest beating resembled that of a gorilla in heat. There were times he pounded one fist near his heart, saying the same thing. This was his way of saying I love you. He said this with such emotion I believed him.

Then the unexpected happened. That is when the guttural primordial screams from me echoed down the hall. Jude was about to rescue me; she never heard this before. But Hans said, "Adam would never hurt her."

These sounds always accompanied love making and occurred at no other time. Adam was a gentle lover at first, but the sounds made him feel as if a fire and its flames were burning at the core of his existence. The noises were disturbing, but only excited Adam more.

Now the wild animal had burst from its cage. It would devour the psyche, confuse and tempt with out of control, psychotic sensual characteristics. Now there was no escaping; the trap was set and he stepped right in. There was no going back.

Adam was quite the adventure. I was at the beginning of a full-blown psychotic episode when I met him. He was a strong, extremely good-looking man with an athletic build. He told me wherever he went, he had a bed. He must have had a lot of friends or girlfriends. He had fancy clothing and many gold chains hanging from his neck. His eyes were like a looking glass; you only saw your likeness, no communication in them. He was definitely a world traveler. Who knows, he could've been a drug lord, but I doubt it. This was something I thought was true at the time!

It was party time, so we ventured to a nightspot with wild, crazy music. Adam bought me a rose and put the stem in his mouth. The flower lay on his cheek. He had a wild look in his eyes as we sipped our drinks. Jude snapped a photo of his hand on my breast in a public restaurant. Oh, I forgot—this was Europe not the United States!

Most of the time anything went. Our hotel pool was topless; even woman in their sixties bared their breasts. Of course I wasn't shy but Jude would have no part in this. In a carnal voice Adam said, "Let's take a stroll outside, Susan."

We walked into the night and then he stopped. A roaring lioness appeared before him. There was no stopping him now.

The night air had a slightly gentle ocean wind, blowing at my side, but not enough to put out this fire. Being psychotic, I'm sure I instigated him further. We both went up in blazes.

I remember that night clearly. There was no sky, only stars. The only thing I could hear was his rapid breathing, then a shout as he gasped for air. "Susan, I never had sex like this in all my life! I love you, Love Baby!"

After this encounter we walked slowly to the bar and danced the rest of the evening.

In a serious voice Hans asked, "Where were you?"

Adam was so fixed in the moment he could scarcely reply. He said something to Hans in German. This was surely a night to remember. This was the first time I saw something in his eyes. He was unable to distinguish these feelings; the driving force of madness and its relentless hunger; I was more than happy to show him the way.

After a night on the town, Hans and Adam always brought Jude and me back safely to our hotel. But the last night, Adam wanted me to stay the night at his place and sleep beside him. I was unable to sleep. My emotions were starting to break through; when I asked him to take me to my hotel he couldn't understand why and seemed disappointed. This was too intimate, lying close to him and feeling a part of him, when I knew the reality: he would be out of my life forever.

Just a bit of reality was peeking through and it hurt. He was unaware of what was going on in my head at this time. He wanted affection that night and I was unable to give it. He was starting to have feelings for me. There were no feelings to give back. I only had glimpses of clarity; I was an animal acting on impulse only. How sad, that madness doesn't love; every two seconds sex, not love, is its pursuit.

Jude had boiled some water to make coffee. I would only drink bottled water, but I had a cup, thinking it was safe. The very next day I had diarrhea. The only thing I drank was soda. I was losing weight rapidly and becoming dehydrated; my skin resembled that of a crocodile.

We were to have dinner with Hans and Adam one evening. They served fresh vegetables and marinated chicken. It was a bit spicy but not too much, just right. Hans was the cook and Adam served the meal; it was delicious.

I ate little and had one glass of wine. It was time for our erotic dance and it was no ballet; a tango, focused on sensuality, was more like it. We kissed. I thought he would yank my lips into his lungs and my tongue along with it. Within moments our clothes went soaring, airborne, in flight, landing on the floor.

I was so excited by now you'd swear there was a tidal wave inside. I became unraveled, bursting with pleasure. This would ignite primeval behavior with aftershocks of an eight on the Richter scale.

Now he was in another world all his own. My inner world was already established years ago, possessing volcanic eruptions of pure pleasure that were not of this world. These sounds were kept at bay, but they turned into voices that haunted me for another decade, until the unholy had the ability to speak.

Later, I found myself outside in the yard with just my underwear. Our friends took a picture. That's when Adam said, "Susan, once again, come to Bangkok with me!" When I got home I blew up the photograph and sent it to him; I still have it.

I thought again about going, but Jude wouldn't be there. Without Jude, I might as well get it over with and shoot myself. I declined his proposal. He said he was going to the go-go lounge there. He was very excited when he mentioned this. It must be quite a loose place, I am quite sure of that.

I had his post card translated in 2012 by my sister Doris's friend, who spoke German and could translate. Adam said he rode elephants, ate on floating restaurants and of course, he loved me. He also gave his regards to Jude. He was unaware at this time that she had died.

He was living through the same intensity that I recognized. Guttural sounds and howling initiated deep inside me again. He became Don Juan, the famous lover.

He was a lost soul now. It was beyond his understanding, but not mine. This was normal sex multiplied by one thousand, an effect of my illness that increased all my senses. Taste, touch and smell were also heightened. If you had a bowl filled with grass it would taste like caviar.

Now you can see why people stop their medication to feel these extremes. But what goes up must come down. Depression is the price. Multiply your normal depression a thousand times; is it worth it?

My answer today is absolutely not; but back then I would have given the depths my soul for it. You know, go to hell in a hand basket!

Adam knew this was special and a moment to remember because there would be no repetition. We each lived on the other side of the world. Jude had been the photographer. I forced her into it, of course. It was hard for her to say no to me.

Before we left she said, “Susan, we haven’t seen any of the island.”

So we got to do some sightseeing, but not much. Jude seemed disappointed in this area.

I wanted to go to Africa, a small boat ride from the island. She was too frightened and didn’t want to go. Of course I wasn’t scared. So I enjoyed myself with African art from the locals.

I said, “Jude, the next vacation we can do anything you want.”

It was time to go home, a sad moment. I would miss Adam; I would miss our crazy nights and wild days filled with ecstasy and craving to be one. Our holiday in the Canary Islands was over but my memories would last forever.

After our trip I enrolled in the fine arts/visual arts program in Berkshire Community College in Pittsfield, Massachusetts and carved our adventures on plates that became a series of etchings. Most are black and white but there are some with color.

On the way home Jude and I were headed for JFK airport in New York City, a thirteen hour flight home. Unfortunately, there was a gigantic snowstorm. When we reached JFK airport, no planes were flying.

However, the airport prepared buses to take us to our next destination, Albany airport.

When we arrived, there was no guarantee that the buses would take us home. I said in an anxious voice, “Jude, we are getting out of here.”

She replied in a sad voice, “Don’t leave me here, Susan.”

“Don't worry, Jude, we’re going home together.”

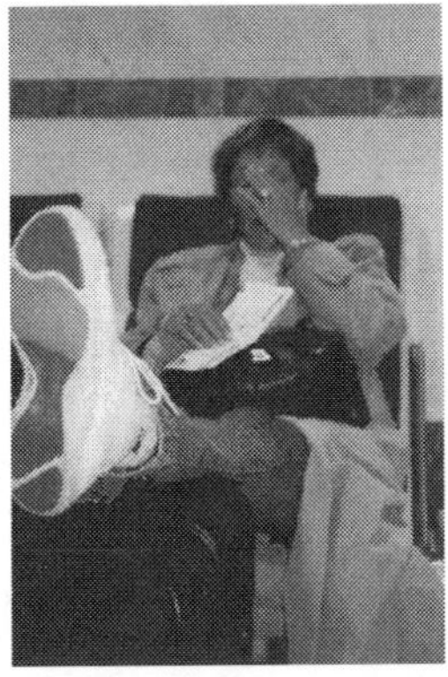

I strolled up to the woman in charge at the arrival gate and said in a stern voice, "Do you know what Manic Depression is? Do you know the meaning? Suicide."

In a flash she was gone. She came back and brought me to her superior. Today they would have taken me away in hand cuffs and put me in jail. I can't believe this was me, no fear of the consequences of my actions. Madness has no boundaries but it was instrumental in getting us out of there.

I said, "Get me to a hospital or a hotel. I can't stay here. I won't get any sleep and without sleep my mental illness will escalate and I will become suicidal. Don't you see this is a medical emergency?"

Immediately after this she brought me to her supervisor, who said in an unsteady voice, "Didn't you tell her a small four engine plane is leaving here in two hours, arriving at Albany Airport at 11 P.M.?" She started to print out a ticket for me.

I said in an imposing voice, "I must have another ticket, my nurse has to go with me or I'll get lost when I reach my destination at Albany airport in Massachusetts."

She gave me two tickets and I went to tell Jude about the good news. She was overjoyed to hear we would be going home together.

When Jude saw a small two engine plane she said in a shrill voice, "We're going to die."

There were two big plows clearing the runway. I didn't see anything problematic. Of course, I was unsound and had no distress, but she was petrified. As we entered the plane, I went to the very back. I had no terror. Jude did, though; she was dealing with a full deck. I didn't even belt-in; I lay down where there were three belts for three seats.

Was I out of my mind? Of course I was, the only one aboard the plane laughing with a smile on her face and making jokes: "Don't worry, we're all going to heaven, just repent and say you're sorry."

No one laughed; it wasn't funny. Madness has its advantages; no brain, no pain. It's floating on a cloud out there somewhere, fluctuating and detached from reality.

It was a rough ride but at last we safely reached our destination, Albany airport. Now another dilemma; our limo wouldn't pick us up. I got another brainstorm. I would call Al and ask him to pick us up; he had a truck. Al liked Jude. He'd met her at the dance he and I attended regularly.

Al said in a sly voice, "If Jude goes to dinner with me I'll pick you up."

Her answer was yes. Al said, "Great, I am on my way."

Al arrived and put our suitcases in the back of his truck. He brought us home safely and the next night Jude went out to dinner with him. He liked Jude and now he had the opportunity to be alone with her.

Nothing much came from the relationship. She lived in Gloucester and he lived in Pittsfield. Long distance relationships rarely work anyway, so neither of them tried.

This whole incident happened fourteen years ago. They probably would've arrested me today after I said "I'm suicidal, get me on a plane," in quite a demanding way.

Of course I was psychotic at the time and didn't realize the consequences of my actions. Sometimes I shudder at my behavior at the airport and what could've happened. But I must say, I had them in the palm of my hand.

That was one crazy night, but being psychotic and having no fear got us home. You had to be insane that night to fly in a blizzard. But I wasn't afraid; my brain was on another frequency! Wow, what a feeling! Madness does have its rewards.

A few weeks after I arrived home, I received a post card in German from Bangkok. The English translation was *I love you, My Love Baby.* I still have that post card. It's in my family bible with photos of my adventures. Some photos are too revealing, so I ripped them into pieces and threw them away.

Little did we know this would be the next to last trip in 2004 in Mexico; she was to die soon after our trip.

Much later I went to a meeting of a singles club at the Williamstown Inn. People in Europe react to situations differently than people in the USA. Like Adam and Hans would always say, "No problem" to everything. They also would click their beer mugs together saying, "Only pigs drink alone."

I wasn't quite sure what this referred to. Americans were more negative and everyone had a problem. The Austrians had a different outlook, that everything was positive and nothing was problematic or a concern. These people knew how to live.

This was my kind of life and I wanted more, but there was no comparison on this evening at the Williamstown Inn. And there was no one there half as exciting as Adam. Nobody at this table had those qualities. Everyone was so boring and it felt like I was at a funeral. Life seemed so humdrum here at home. I was high on life and people back home were mind numbingly zombielike. Now things were going to get chaotic, because I was on a role and so was my mouth. There was no stopping me.

The women were talking about drapes and wallpaper, stupid stuff as far as I was concerned. With a loud voice I burst out the words, "You're tensile people from Tinsel town. When are you going to learn how to live, when you're fucking dead?"

All my life I had a zest for life—more than anyone that I knew, that is. Being psychotic amplified my offensive psychotic attitude and conduct. No one knew I was psychotic. They thought I was drunk out of my mind. Now I was out of control and definitely psychotic, insulting everyone beyond words. I wasn't drinking; not a drop of alcohol touched my lips but they thought I was drunk because of my manners.

In a revolting voice this woman said, “You can't say fuck in my town.”

With a loud, irate voice I replied, “I can say whatever I want and any place I want.”

I saw a young police officer ordering coffee to bring back to the police station. The police station was right in back of the hotel.

I asked, “Mister Police officer, can I say fuck in this hotel?”

He replied, “Of course you can.”

This was all I needed, permission from an officer of the law. I shouted from the bar, “See, I told you I could say fuck.”

Then I threw my arms around a gay waiter and in a dramatized voice I said,” I love you.” I believe I was getting closer and closer to getting arrested.

My friend said, “We have to go and now.” If it weren’t for him I probably would have been arrested for disturbing the peace.

I found negatives of the Canary Islands and the romantic love afire that Adam and I had. One photo was of Adam and me kissing, an etching I did in college.

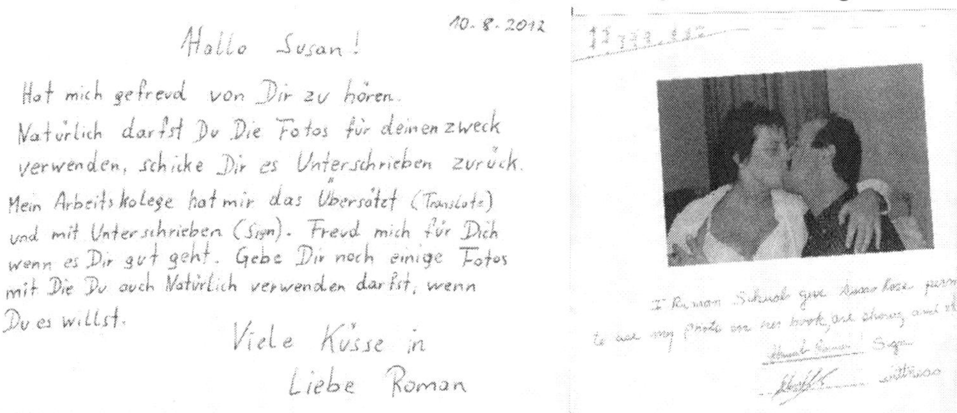

10. 8. 2012

Hallo Susan!

Hat mich gefreud von Dir zu hören.
Natürlich darfst Du Die Fotos für deinen zweck verwenden, schicke Dir es Unterschrieben zurück.
Mein Arbeitskolege hat mir das Übersötet (Translate) und mit Unterschrieben (Sign). Freud mich für Dich wenn es Dir gut geht. Gebe Dir noch einige Fotos mit Die Du auch Natürlich verwenden darfst, wenn Du es willst.

Viele Küsse in
Liebe Roman

The other day I found an old address book in my attic. It was a hundred degrees up there. The sweat trickled downward into my eyes and I was wiping them in order to see.

Adam’s work number was there. I gave it a call; it just rang. Nobody answered. Then my phone rang. I picked it up. I heard a cheerful loud voice say “Sue san, Su san.”

He could not pronounce my name correctly, “Susan.”

I asked him permission to use our photograph in my book. I sent the photograph and permission slip for him to sign. In about ten days I had received a permission slip from him and witnessed it. He also sent photographs that I didn't have and permission for those to be used also, if needed. Now I was stable and not clearly out of my mind like I was in the Canary Islands when we first met in the xyear2000!

I received so much joy listening to his laughter in the background; suddenly I was in the Canary Islands again. I shared some of this story on a cable television show in the year 2012. I was so excited talking about this story I felt like I was there.

Jude said, "Susan, live with me; take two years and your life will go in the right direction." But this would not happen.

One time, when Jude and I returned from a vacation early, we flirted with a waiter Yes, I won. However, I never slept with him. This was more like a game we were playing.

Jude sometimes called me a "Walking Vagina." I wasn't offended because it was the truth. Observing my sexually repulsive conduct in the past makes me feel ashamed and humiliated. The person back then wasn't me. Yet it was an everyday occurrence and I have to accept my past.

Jude liked men, but never married. One time when we were in our fifties she was visiting me. We went out to a local hotel bar. She got drunk. I never saw her this way before; I never knew her to have a problem with alcohol.

She became loud and we left. It was quite embarrassing but nothing close to my moments of madness.

Because it was winter, my steep stairs were very icy and slippery. They constantly needed sanding because the water on the roof dripped, making the first step form into ice.

One time it was so thick I went out there with a pick axe and slag hammer. What a sight to see! Everyone knew I was crazy and I surely looked like it, swinging a pick axe in the air. No one called the cops; this was nothing out of the ordinary for crazy Sue! If it was anybody else, there would be a 911 call.

Jude took one step and then sat down. She was laughing and paid no attention to what I was saying. It wasn't easy getting her up each stair. When we reached the porch she kissed me passionately, though she wasn't gay. This didn't bother me. At the time she was plastered.

The next morning, I mentioned the incident. She said, "You shouldn't talk about it or bring it up the next day, Susan."

That was the last time we spoke about it. I never questioned her later.

Snorkeling on our next holiday was in Cancun, Mexico. The fish were colorful and so close you could almost touch them. One day, while snorkeling, there was an incident where the guide grabbed me by the crotch. He did it again and again but I said nothing.

When we left I told Jude what had happened. She was furious that I didn't say something. But we were in another country and did not want to tell the authorities.

To this day, I have no idea why he did this. I didn't even speak to the guide; it wasn't my fault. Am I a magnet? Do I have a sign that says walk right in, all welcome?

I am someone people touch freely and I never object. All my life I used to intrude on people's space. While we were talking I would touch them, implying that I was giving them a sexual invitation. This was not always my intent; this was just my nature.

You could call it my manic personality. I made people feel as though I'd known them all my life. Because of that, I felt at ease in places where I knew no one. I made sure I was always the center of attention.

On one of our sightseeing trips, Jude and I went to a Mayan temple in Mexico. There was a huge flight of stairs inside. When we got to the top Jude was gasping for air. I didn't think much of this incident; it was quite a climb. I was out of breath but not like her; I was a non-smoker and had never put a cigarette in my mouth.

When we returned home the doctor said Judith had pneumonia but didn't take an x-ray. If an x-ray had been taken they would have seen the early stages of cancer and could have saved her life.

Time went by and I said to Jude with concern, "Jude, your voice, it's like you have laryngitis. You should see a doctor. And why is there blood in your urine?"

But she didn't go until it was too late.

I visited Jude for two weeks before she died. I was always afraid of getting lost, especially on long distance destinations. So every summer my son Jack would drive me there. One summer Jude said, "You can drive, Susan. I know you can do it."

So I wrote out directions and put them on the front seat. That turned out to be a bad place because I had to keep looking down. I was nervous all the way there but the trip went smoothly. Then, when I was only a mile from her house and there was just one more stop light and… I looked down. I hit the curb, blew out both tires and just made it to Jude's front door.

Fortunately the gas station Jude frequently used wasn't the type to overcharge.

The mechanic put on two new tires and charged me nothing for labor, considering the tires I blew out were absolutely brand new.

Every day we went to Jude's favorite restaurant for lunch and she ordered two vodka gimlets. She always sat in the same seat and said it was because her favorite waitress was there. The waitress would hand her a bag and they would exchange money. Now I knew Jude was buying pot. I had some years ago and I hated the way it made me feel, but Jude smoked it often.

Jude was so patient with her mother, who had Alzheimer's. One day when her mom's cousins were painting the house, Betty asked, "Jude, who is painting the house?"

Jude replied, "Your cousins, Betty."

Two seconds later Betty would ask again who was painting the house.

After two years Betty's Alzheimer's was so severe she had to be put in the local nursing facility in Gloucester. Jude never missed a day going to see her mom.

When I visited Jude we brought her mom a milkshake every afternoon. Jude never called her "mom." She always called her by her first name, "Betty." That seemed a little strange; though I'm sure Jude had her reasons.

Betty and Jude loved animals. Between them they had five cats. Every time we came to visit Betty, we put the TV on the animal channel. She always asked, "When am I going home?"

I can't remember Jude's exact reply but she always told her mom she would be leaving soon.

Betty must have asked 100 times, "When am I going home?"

"Soon," Jude kept saying, even though it wasn't true.

Peter came into my life just in time. I can't say he took her place, or he became a substitute; no one could replace her. I'd known Peter for a year before he brought me back and forth to Gloucester during Jude's fight with death. During that year Peter hadn't changed much; he still wore ragged clothes and looked unkempt. Jude and Bob felt uneasy letting Peter stay overnight so he slept under a bridge.

When Judith was recently diagnosed and still mobile I said in an uplifting voice, "Let me take you to dinner tonight."

The route we took went by the bridge where Peter was staying. We were on a two-lane highway but I wanted to stop and see how Peter was doing. Jude wasn't happy about this but I told her I wouldn't stay for long.

I jumped the guard rail and slowly went down the embankment. Peter was sitting peacefully with the fire cooking something in his makeshift stove. I was surprised how warm it was under the bridge.

"We're going out to dinner," I said as I kissed him and gave him a hug. "Pleasant dreams, my love."

I scurried up the side of the embankment and jumped over the guard rail. Then I opened the car door and began to drive while Jude tried her best to discourage me about Peter. But my ears were closed shut to any demanding that I leave my hobo.

Jude was my only friend, always there for me. Now it was my turn to be there for her. I tried to take my life once more.

Jude, my friend of thirty years, was in the hospital, dying. She had small cell carcinoma which was untreatable. When I arrived at her home I knocked at her door. As she opened it, she said the heart stopping words "I'm a dead women and I did it to myself."

The doctor said, "You have one and a half months to live." I can't imagine the panic these words scratched into her brain, setting it on fire.

It was a result of smoking. She told me, "I'm afraid of dying."

After learning this news, a rush of pain vibrated through my body as if an owl had taken its talons and ripped my heart out.

I gently asked her, "What did you ever do in your life that was an act so evil it would send you to hell?"

Hell was real to her; she believed this existed. Every time we passed a church she would make the sign of the cross.

She responded, "Nothing."

Then I asked her, "Then what do you have to be worried about? As I recall, your life was pure as snow, especially compared to mine."

If anyone was going to hell it was me, breaking almost every commandment. I was Catholic also and as a youngster I was indoctrinated with fear rather than love.

As a kid, the anxiety of going to hell and suffering time without end was very real. As a child I was scared to death, indoctrinated with the fear of God. You couldn't think a bad thought; that was a sin.

You couldn't even think! Isn't that crazy, you couldn't even think? It's impossible. I have spent many years trying to undo these teachings, with some success.

Jude, on the other hand, was a strong believer, so I comforted her as best I could, to conquer her distress of hell and damnation. I think I was successful in diminishing her worry.

I felt so helpless. There wasn't much time left. She only had a month and a half to live and two weeks had already passed. I took her out to dinner that night and she ordered surf-n-turf with two vodka gimlets. I thought this would be our last dinner together and I was right.

We walked to the car. As she entered the passenger side she stopped. Almost in tears she said with alarm, "My leg, I can't lift my leg."

She had to manually lift the leg, using her hand, as she entered the car on the passenger side. After she fastened her seat belt, she turned and when our eyes met I saw extreme panic.

She said, "Susan, the cancer has gone to my brain; my leg, it won't move, they're right, my time is up."

She was right. The right leg was starting to swell and turned blue. In time it turned an ugly black color, indicating no circulation of blood. It is a good thing she died soon. I don't know if they would have amputated in this circumstance.
There were stairs to climb at home and eventually she was to stay in a nursing home until her death. She asked me to wash her rather than the nurse. This made me feel like I had some control over my own fears and feelings of helplessness concerning her death. I would always stay until she went to sleep and kiss her forehead when I left. She looked like an angel. She wanted me to put her coat on, push her in a wheelchair, and bring her outside to smoke a cigarette.

What harm could smoking do? She only had two months left and her cancer was terminal. If she wanted to smoke a whole pack it was fine with me. We only smoked one or two cigarettes and went back to the warmth of her room. It was early spring and cold outdoors and that stopped us from smoking long periods.

Jude sobbed, "I just want to see spring."

But she died just before spring, as the trees were starting to bud. You know the rest of the story. Jude called me frequently when she was in the hospital, saying the doctor told her she might not make it through the night. So in the morning I'd drive to Gloucester, stay at her home and sleep in her bed. I did this four times before the end.

Jude lived with her younger brother Bob. He was kind of nervous but was always gracious and kind to me. She had another brother, Joseph, who lived in North Carolina. They had a somewhat tense relationship.

But that all changed when she was dying; there was no time for petty grievances. Joseph rented a vehicle while staying with Jude and every evening, before going to see Jude, he brought Bob and me to many fine restaurants.

In one conversation Joseph and Jude made amends and they said to each other, "I love you."

On one visit when Jude was first hospitalized Joseph took a video of her friends and brother discussing a TV host show from years ago. Everybody was guessing the host's name; of course I was wrong.

I remember Jude saying, "You could screw up a free lunch."

I remember that and start to laugh. She could never offend me. It makes me sad to remember the events preceding her death. I recently turned the video into a CD.

It was beyond both of our imaginations that Jude would one day be dying of small cell carcinoma in the same nursing facility as her mother. We never imagined having to tell Betty that Jude was fading fast… then gone forever.

Jude came home after her hospital stay but the stairs were an obstacle. The nursing home was her only choice. The horrible irony was her mother had been a resident there for two years and now her daughter had arrived.

Sadness overcame me when I wheeled Judith down to her mom's room to explain that she would die soon. How to get this across to her mom with end-stage Alzheimer's? I think it was a miracle.

Although the words "Mom, I'm dying" didn't work the emotions sparked small amount of clarity.

Betty understood, but just for a few seconds before she was back to oblivion.

Whoever thought that Betty, with end-stage Alzheimer's, would live and her daughter would die before her? Sometimes Alzheimer's is a blessing instead of a curse, especially in this case. Betty attended the funeral but I didn't see any sign that she knew what was happening. Two years later Betty succumbed to pneumonia.

On March 7, 2005, Jude's brother called and told me she had passed that night. When she took her last breath, the nurses draped her in my prayer shawl. Her spirit must have passed through and left its shadow imprisoned between its threads.

The shawl hangs on a hook in my bedroom, under her picture. I wore it once at a synagogue service than placed it back on its hook. It hangs there still. I no longer practice this religion but I believe there is a God.

I have so many warmhearted memories, especially of her well-known sarcastic wit, which I took no offense to.

Jude was my lifelong friend and I lost her. I could hardly stand the agony within me. What would I do without her? There was no one else, nor would there be in my future. I had to face that I was to be alone. Our time was up.

She said if I was dying she couldn't bear it and felt glad it was her instead. She never veered from my side, even in my most irrational moments. If not for her, I would have made more blunders in my life, which would have caused even more pain.

There was a small service at the grave site and a reception at a nearby restaurant, where friends and family could pay their respects. Jude had collected an enormous amount of jewelry: one hundred rings, necklaces, bracelets and chains. Everyone had a preference; some took rings and others took different pieces. Before her death, she gave me diamond heart shaped earrings that she wanted me to have.

Jude was cremated and put in a white ceramic urn, which was placed in her family burial plot. Her uncle had a bouquet of red roses and handed them out to the people that attended. I put my rose on her urn then bent down and touched my warm lips in a final kiss against the cold porcelain positioned in the ice cold grave, never to embrace her warm body again. This was my way of saying farewell.

Oh, how I loved her! Her presence is never-ending in my thoughts, not letting go.

Jude never left my side, even in my most insane antics. She died with grace. What a priceless woman. I appreciated respected and valued her until the unpleasant end. Jude was a big part of my recovery from madness to sanity. Her love was my drug but not a remedy. I had fallen back far into madness, to return in any hurried fashion and it had a firm grip on me. The stress related to her death hospitalized me with a setback.

At one point I was going to live with Jude and her brother for two years. I needed time to get my life together, away from my children. Jude passed away before this could happen.

There was a very strong bond between us. We loved one another so much and trusted each other implicitly. This kind of friendship only comes along once in a lifetime… if you're lucky, that is. She was my lucky star!

"S" For Suicide/ Hospital

THE DEMONS ARE WITHIN

My very first thoughts of suicide were at age twelve. I rode my bike across the river to my nana's house. I stopped many times halfway, parked my bike and put the kick stand down to keep the bike upright.

Stepping closer, I bent at the waist to see the river. There was a massive stone-walled barrier. My brain contemplated the conclusion of jumping to my death.

Why did this bottomless, murky river beckon me? The dread of high elevations scared me and stopped the jump. Heights were fear-provoking and made me feel close to fainting.

In 1968, when I was eighteen and Luke was twenty, I tried to jump from a moving car. My two-year-old son Eugene was in the back seat with my mother-in law Eva. Luke was driving the car. We had a disagreement that almost ended with my body parts scattered, along the roadside.

"Stop the car and let me out!" I yelled.

He didn't, so I yelled again, "Stop the car now!"

He paid no attention. I went for the door with my right hand, grabbed the lever and opened the door.

There I was, upset and prepared to jump. Eva grabbed my forearm. She was a strong women and dragged me back into the moving car, saving me from an untimely death because I was about to become road kill.

Can you see the crows circling me, waiting to pick my bones clean? Or a worse outcome was to be crippled and lying in a heap. This was an impulsive act.

My first hospital stay in 1987 had no psychiatric diagnosis. What a pity. If caught early, I would not have endured such an extended period of time recovering. But there was no medication ordered. No diagnosis was made other than "an attempted suicide with a butcher knife."

If I was treated with medication in the beginning, I may have avoided the massive psychotic break in 1989 that took everything I loved: my children, my marriage, my job, my health, my home and a son to prison for a crime he never committed.

After discharge, I was to make an appointment with my therapist and I did. I had a good therapist but she couldn't see I was in deep trouble. Come on, you don't have to be a rocket scientist! A butcher knife held over my head, coming down on my wrist—who would catch the severed hand, Dr. Frankenstein? He could use it.

Even when I had the break my therapist could not see it and with conviction she said, "All you need is a bandage."

A Band-Aid! If I completed the task we would need a tourniquet. Was everyone blind?

In 1989 I spent two and a half months in a locked ward, after months with hardly any sleep, hallucinating, not eating, bizarre behavior and sexually out-of-control. I was about to run myself into the ground. I was malnourished and dehydrated, wringing myself out like an old dish rag. This was an unknown suicide in the making. Someone else needed to intervene, or I was a goner.

Eight years later I attempted suicide again. I was in a rocky relationship with Dave. We were at his mother's house and I was suspicious about his faithfulness in our relationship. An argument ensued, leading to another suicide attempt on my part.

I decided to take a walk to a pond where a family of ducks lived. I wasn't thinking about suicide or how to do it, but the fog invaded me and turned me into only a hazy puff as I was walking back.

My drug of choice for overdose was a benzodiazepine. It reduced panic attacks and slowed down my racing mind. The first thing I saw was my anxiety pills. On impulse I calmly released them into my empty hand, as though nothing was wrong. I swallowed them all: Chug-a-lug! David was startled. It was his turn to act. Destination: hospital. Dave drove me to there. Time to drink the charcoal!

Another trigger was one of the times Jack was angry with me. A situation concerning my moral behavior in the past had surfaced. Jack's father conveyed bald-faced lies about me when Jack was twelve. Jack had believed me before, but as an adult he questioned me. This was no surprise; I knew this would materialize, so I always spoke the truth. But now this harmed me as an individual.

Yes! Suicide, here I come!

This was a wound with no validity but it had sufficient power to create dissociation. The fog disconnected me. There I was again, a handful of pills down the hatch. The ambulance came and brought me to the hospital; then I was swallowing a full cup of charcoal. God I hated that stuff! I always reached the emergency room without becoming unconscious.

Over the course of ten years, I drank so much charcoal I could have heated my house with it.

My therapist at the time said, "Put a big S on your refrigerator. You will see it and say to yourself, Do I feel like this? If it's yes, call the crisis unit."

The S stood for Suicide. A cup of charcoal wasn't a large enough deterrent to stop me from taking my life. But knowing what dissociation felt like stopped my suicide attempts. Suicidal feelings were hard for me to detect but when I knew this monster, it lost its power.

2003 found me in the emergency room trying to hang myself with rubber tubing. Today I'm thinking it was ridiculous. Now, the plastic bag in the wastepaper basket, that's a thought! I could put it over my head and suffocate. If I was wearing sneakers I could have hung myself with the laces.

Every emergency room should have a safe area for suicidal patients. When you're put in a cell as a prisoner they take your laces. What's wrong with that picture?

PARANOIA STRIKES

After my mother-in-law died, I inherited thousands of dollars of gold jewelry and diamond earrings. I hid them all over the house and then forgot where they were.

This jewelry was also to get money if I needed it for my divorce. I saw a suspicious card my husband received from an admirer. I wanted to read it and he was reluctant to let me.

He had it in his upper left pocket on his shirt. He had no choice; he was caught red-handed, or so I thought. He reached into his pocket and handed it to me.

The writer described Isaac in a feminine way. I was so paranoid I read it over and over a thousand times; paranoia run riot. They say sometimes there is truth to paranoia and I was bent on finding it. I brought the card, evidence I was sure, to my therapist.

She said in a serious voice, "Reading it, it's not enough to hang him."

This still didn't stop me from reading it over and over. I was convinced it was true. This wasn't normal paranoia; it was connected to insanity too intense to define.

Paranoia didn't stop in 1989 with my psychotic break. I even suffer today at a low intensity. For instance I'm 100% sure someone I know is getting into my computer.

In the early '90s I worked at Willowood, a small nursing facility in the beautiful blue hills of North Adams. My paranoia was present exactly in the middle, not extremely high, certainly not low.

One incident that stands out in my mind is a time I had a nightmare that someone was going to kill me and surrounded my bed with 18 steak knives. Then I thought, *I must barricade the door.*

I took a chair and put it underneath the doorknob but I still wasn't satisfied. I took an antique table and placed it against the door instead. I still didn't feel safe.

This type of thinking went on for quite a long time. I have old note books with passages about my paranoia. In October of 1994 I had only two good days where I slept, but I still had weird dreams.

In one dream a man with dark rimmed glasses, who I knew from childhood, was staring at me. I think he was the insurance man; in those days they came to the house to collect monthly payments. I'd always been afraid of him. He gave me candy. Mom told me never to accept candy from strangers, but he wasn't a stranger.

In June of 1996 I was still afraid someone wanted to do me harm. An odd phone call from a man with a young sounding voice frightened me. He said, "I'm doing a survey of the neighborhood about smoking cigarettes and how many people in the neighborhood smoked."

I replied, "I don't smoke." But when I got off the phone paranoia struck like a lightning bolt. I had told him I lived alone. My name was the only one in the telephone book with the last name "Rose." Was he stalking me?

Another time I was convinced my boyfriend was cheating on me. Before he went to work I put a tape recorder in his pocket and listened to it when he came home. The recordings were vague but I was so paranoid I listened to it over and over again, taking it apart to look for evidence that wasn't there. I smelled his shirts, jackets and underwear; my craziness had no bounds. I was using up all my energy trying to find proof of his infidelity.

Finally my therapist told me with conviction, "Stop this. Susan, his ugly head will pop up someday and then he will be accusing you."

Though this kind of thinking continued for four more years, her advice helped to decrease the paranoia that I was experiencing.

Sometimes I think back to those days when pain consumed me and I wonder how I can get frazzled with the small stuff that life deals you. I had been to hell and its demons tried to possess me, but I found my way back to a godly terrain.

"When you look into an abyss, the abyss also looks into you."
--Friedrich Nietzsche

"The cradle rocks above an abyss and common sense tells us that our existence is but a brief crack of light between two eternities of darkness."
--Vladimir Nabokov

My life was out-of-control and my AA sponsor, Todd, would be instrumental in admitting me to the psychiatric ward of Brookside hospital in New Hampshire. I would be there for months.

One recollection during the journey was of uncontrollable laughter. During admission they asked me to count; this was a task I was incapable of doing. I was not able to spit out the number one, that's the God awful truth.

The medications made my face became expressionless. When walking, I shuffled my feet like those of an old man and never blinked my eyes, just constantly stared.

My roommate was Sally, a young girl with long blond hair and a slim figure. Sally had studied theology for the last two years. She was always pessimistic. Her mental illness affected her with disorganized thinking, jumping from one subject to another.

Subject jumping and responding "Yes" then "No" then "Yes" again was called repetitive behavior. It was familiar. I called it my flip-flop mind.

Sally was an excellent roommate. Although restless, she was harmless. Sometimes she said, "This hell and brimstone makes me crazy; I can't get it out of my head. Susan, find a king-size eraser and erase hell's despicable chains adhering to my brain."

"I don't think it'll work," I said.

Sally actually believed it could; that's the creepy part. Also she was hearing noises that adhered to her brain. Who knows if she made it out of there?

In the hospital, we had to stay in our room and out of others. There were males on the ward, stealing was a problem and of course safety was a reason.

A tall lanky man, an ugly cuss with jet-black hair, stood at the threshold of my room and gawked at me. He resembled President Lincoln. He had no idea why my door was open. Being an attention-seeker, I was standing there in my underwear, naked and unashamed, not me. I am mortified at the memory. Rules? I had none and didn't abide by the hospital's. I walked into males' rooms without any announcement.

One time I walked in a man's room and pulled my skirt over my head. He was young and didn't see me. He was in his own universe, striking the closet door so hard his fists dripped of blood. I wanted to block my ears, unable to stop the sounds pulsating in my eardrums.

We were on a locked ward but one man wanted out. There were two doors that met in the middle. He casually walked to the door, gave it a devastating blow with his booted foot and it flew open. Out he went in a blaze of fury. Watching this was scary. The hospital became an unsafe dwelling.

"What would you do, Susan, if you felt rage?" a curious nurse asked.

"I possessed rage. Recalling its mighty power, I chased my children in a rage up a flight of stairs in our home and they hid in the bathroom locking themselves in and would not open the door; that was how afraid they were of me. I remember banging on the door with my fist, screaming, but I don't remember the words. When they sensed no danger they came out. I was calm and they felt it was safe. This only happened once. I have no idea what I was capable of if I caught them. But even you possess this demon, only at a reduced level of intensity, Nurse Nancy."

My rage is different in the respect that it is quicker to ignite and harder to arrest. Make no mistake. It lies dormant, this demon and I must be vigilant. The term I give rage is **I see red!**

Doctor Hyde diagnosed me upon admission. I was sitting in a chair and my whole body felt numb.

In a solemn voice he said, "You have Bipolar Disorder. What a shame. Not knowing this in your youth, your intelligence level is so high, the ability to achieve great things was in your grip."

"Will my sons get this Bipolar disorder?" I nervously asked.

"No, mostly girls do." Boy was he wrong; all four of my sons inherited it.

I was happy to hear a diagnosis after my suffering, better described as fighting the three-headed dogs at the gates of hell. Having a name for it helped. I was healed!

Not that fast. Complete cure, never. Just less pain as time passed.

Was my analogy wrong? Was this invitation to hell? My bewildering spiritual journey began, to restore this shattered spirit that dwelled within me. There were times I felt no physical body, only a vessel filled with agony.

Even with medication my sleep habits stayed the same. No sleep, my mind a reckless train running out of control. My body was skeleton-like and I had no craving for food. But I would recover if I could slumber once again. Each sunset I imagined this could be the night I would rest. I kept waiting for daybreak to allow my sleepless nights to evaporate. Madness took eons to become real.

When Eugene brought me to the movie "Alien" on a day pass, I almost jumped out of my skin. I couldn't sit still. Too much stimulation. I was so uncomfortable I felt like a jumping bean was encased in my skin and a snake in my ass, slithering side to side.

When I left the hospital even the supermarket was too much all at once—a scary place, too hard to handle. It made me uneasy, but as time passed I became acclimated.

There would be nine more hospitalizations for me, although I can't recall them all. Talking about them is not as difficult as I thought it would be. A stretch of time has passed and it seems as though this never happened, as if I were telling someone else's story.

It took a while to get to the hospital ward but when I arrived, I stayed in my room unless we had activities. I wasn't very sociable and didn't make friends. They were strangers with the brain virus. It seemed like a virus; everyone had it. This was my metaphor for BPD. But this virus wasn't catchy, even though when discussing it with others they backed away like it was. They didn't want to hear it; they were afraid that madness might snatch their minds someday and they'd become like me: the mad hatter, living in Alice in Wonderland world.

I never had any visits from my sons and I liked it that way. I needed a rest; all their hurtful behavior put me in the hospital. I stayed in my room, came out for meals and attended everything scheduled that day. If there was an unoccupied room I jumped at the opportunity and always observed the rules, so nursing staff felt comfortable and accommodated me

There were two beds to a room. If the number of patients increased I had no choice but to get a roommate. Roommates played loud music, were sometimes disagreeable and snored.

My misfortune was not getting a full night's rest. The best medication is sleep and without it other medication has less effectiveness; subsequently, highs and lows will intensify.

I will say it one more time: SLEEP and don't forget, LOVE! It's not a cure but is a great medicine.

I always joined group therapy and art therapy. I never showed arrogance or superiority and never questioned authority. I was easygoing, not a troublemaker. I never smoked cigarettes but other people did. Currently in the psychiatric unit they have "No Smoking" rules. Patients wear nicotine patches for nicotine withdrawal.

In the hospital we had therapy sessions and most people talked, but the doctor refused to let me discuss anything. Storming out of the room was not like me, a model patient never giving anyone trouble during my hospital stays the last years.

The highlights of the day at the hospital were breakfast, lunch and dinner. I could order anything I wanted on the menu; the food was quite good. I only ate one meal a day at home.

I never had many conversations with other patients. Ultimately, friendships never evolved. The hospital stays were usually one week.

I read an article that having a mental illness might take ten years off your lifespan. When I asked the psychiatrist she said, “Most patients with mental illness smoke, drink, do drugs and get into dangerous situations; they have no fear.”

The only thing I could relate to was “no fear.” I didn't smoke, drink or do drugs but I engaged in dangerous situations many, many times. I should be dead. (Was it luck or was there a benevolent presence protecting me?)

Discovering the correct medication is a crapshoot. Everybody is different. Psychiatric medication changes are sometimes hazardous and sanity is in jeopardy. It’s a throw of the dice until an accurate combination of medication works. Even then updates are needed. I encountered this and let me convey, it’s scary. Will the next concoction given work?

When I was admitted to the hospital in 2002, I was psychotic and the medication I was on wasn't working. The doctors wanted to administer Lithium again but I was reluctant to take it. I had discontinued this medication because of severe side effects. My abdomen blew up to four times its size. I resembled a pregnant woman in her third trimester. I had thrush, dry skin, hair loss and intolerable blurry vision. The only side effect I didn’t have was shaky hands.

But the depression and elation weren't going away. It was shock treatments or Lithium or I’d surely kill myself.

What’s worse: the inability to evoke your short term recollections, or taking your life? So I took the latter, Lithium.

The situation at home was a deep blow to my mind and heart. I needed time to recover and talk therapy.

Yes, I had a voice and I used it with policies that were dehumanizing. I recall when my lips were cemented; I was powerless with no defenses. I am somebody to contend with but still total lack of respect goes on, even in safe places. I now have a psychiatrist, Nancy, who respects me and gives me dignity. But I earned it… and that's about all I want to say about that.

I call the first feeling of depression the tip of the iceberg. The hidden part of depression laying beneath the water was enormous and I couldn’t face that monster again. I needed some quiet time to get some kind of balance. I couldn't take antidepressant medication because it would make me manic. I'd rather be manic than depressed but most of my hospitalizations were for mania.

The therapist on call said, "I will admit you. Promise no passes at the men on the ward."

This promise would be an accomplishment to keep.

"No problem," I replied.

I don't think I really meant it. This undertaking was a task that wasn't easy in my condition. Yet the promise was kept and all the men were safe from me. This didn't stop me from flirting, I am sure of that.

I told the nursing staff, "I can't do this again."

The pain I was referring to was the demon in my past, my first depression, sitting in the cellar of lost souls.

They sent me to see the doctor who said, "Susan, you won't go back that far."

This made sense and reassured me. I was released after a week. Life took on a new meaning. I had to fend for myself; no more Jude for the critical experiences that would come to be in my future.

I was in my late fifties before there was any hint of stability. Stability was the key to reduce heightened sexual eagerness but that wouldn't happen until a decade later.

Now it's 2012. I haven't been hospitalized in four years, cutting medications in half. I was too sedated with medication that I no longer require; my life stressors are reduced and high levels of medication no longer necessary. I have clarity now. The last few years I have reclaimed my voice and I am using it. I am truly blessed!

WORK—
A PURPOSE

My reality as a child was being destitute. Mom was like a broken record as she repeated, "We can't afford it."

She went to her grave saying, "We haven't enough money!"

Making a better life for myself was important. No more being poor, having to put cardboard on the sole of my shoes when a hole appeared.

A paycheck was everything to me. That said I was worth something. Isaac always made me feel small and incomplete in so many ways; no matter what I did, it was never enough for his approval. I could stand on my head and spit nickels all day and that wouldn't be enough.

When my son was four years old he went to nursery school during the day. During the weekend, his grandmother looked after him so I could work.

I worked forty hours a week at the hospital with no pay for a year and a half, but lunch was free. I had double of everything.

The cashier asked in a condescending voice, "Will you eat everything?"

I said, "I will eat all I can, bet on that."

She thought I was giving some away. I didn't gain much weight; I ate considerably less during other meals to save money.

For a year I also worked as a cocktail waitress on weekends. I never received big tips, even though the place was packed. Individuals that came dancing hardly ever tipped. The pay was poor, but I needed money for transportation to my job at the hospital.

Although I had an 8-cylinder Chevrolet that never needed repair, it was old and wasn't good on gas.

The waitress job was extra spending money. I received no pay at the hospital because it was considered a training program. I had my welfare check, some money for uniforms and of course free lunch. I took full advantage of that.

There were other mothers working welfare but just a few finished the program. I was determined to finish. Opportunity was knocking and I took it.

We worked days and evenings but there was no night shift yet. We took calls for the night shifts, but only for emergencies. This worked well. We all lived close to the hospital, which made this possible. We had to accept more responsibility and the night shift was born.

This made my job as a waitress impossible so I had to quit. It wasn't too much later that I was hired and received a pay check; my income tripled.

My efforts were starting to materialize. A good paying job and a better life were becoming obvious. This was one of the happier moments in my young life. My twenties were the carefree years. I had no clue what lay ahead in my future—a downhill spiral.

After a year and a half I was hired as a respiratory therapist at Roger William's hospital in Rhode Island. I quit my waitress job because now I was getting paid, filling in on the night shift when someone called in sick. I took all the overtime I could get. My starting wage was $3.25 an hour, a decent salary at the time.

I also took on the responsibility of assistant chief of the respiratory department but it wasn't a salaried job; I was paid by the hour.

I enjoyed working with men more than women. Every night somebody went home early and the other workers took over. We never argued about who would leave.

When I worked with women there was always an argument. "You went home last night." "You went home early three nights this week."

This pettiness didn't happen when I worked with men; I thought more like the men than the women.

At twenty-one I was already second in command. I was someone with self-confidence, something I had never experienced before due to my mental illness and childhood emotional and sexual abuse. I thought my name was "Stupid."

Mother and school teachers constantly called me this. I started to believe what they said and carried this notion to adulthood.

When I was a respiratory therapist I questioned their abuse. Maybe they were wrong. How could I be stupid when this job needed intelligence and a good memory?

When my mental illness crept in the feelings of stupid came back, sometimes with a vengeance. Would I ever feel good about myself? Not if my mental illness had anything to say about it.

When the boss hired me as the assistant chief of respiratory medicine I knew this was a good-paying job and I would not have a second chance. There was no help for pregnant mothers in my generation and I couldn't have a child and then give it up.

My family was no help either; they were poor and had no resources to help me. They barely had enough money to survive.

I would lose the only way to improve my life and my son's. If I was back on the welfare role, my first chance for a good job and a better life would disappear and the future wouldn't be promising.

I took the job and my life took another turn for the best. Working made me feel important and I felt some self-confidence for a change. This job was not like most jobs. I had to deal with life and death every day. The job became like home; that's how much I liked it. I wondered why they paid me. The responsibilities I had that went along with this job made me feel special.

Lou, a patient in his early twenties, made me a red paper flower. He was my age and cursed with Hodgkin's Lymphoma, a death sentence in 1974.

When we saw the movie "Mash" at a drive-in theater he brought a pint of coffee brandy and many sweet kisses; I didn't see much of the movie. There was no sex, just a lot of affection, hugging and holding hands.

I wasn't pleased with the way I handled the situation. I feel I could have been more sympathetic. Lou and I went to lunch and talked about his dreams and how college and a good job awaited him.

But there would be no college for him. I was not God, but death was closing in on him and fast. I knew it but he had no idea. I was helpless in this situation, yet I never spoke a word about him having no future. Was he in denial? Did the doctors not inform him of his impending demise?

One Monday morning I found he'd died that weekend. I was thankful I was not there. My biggest regret is that I wasn't there to comfort him in his last moments. I still feel a coward with minimal feelings.

Throughout my 32 years working, many times I asked my patients, "How did you handle tough times throughout your life? Tell me your secret."

Each person told a different story of a time when they had handled tough times, some using witticism and others using wisecracks.

One older gentleman laid motionless, eyes closed. He appeared comatose. I was sure he would not reply but with incredible strength, he recited the poem "IF" by Rudyard Kipling.

If
By Rudyard Kipling

If you can keep your head when all about you
Are losing theirs and blaming it on you,
If you can trust yourself when all men doubt you,
But make allowance for their doubting too;
And yet don't look too good, nor talk too wise:
If you can dream and not make dreams your master;
If you can think and not make thoughts your aim;
If you can meet with Triumph and Disaster
And treat those two impostors just the same;

If you can bear to hear the truth you've spoken
Twisted by knives to make a trap for fools,
Or watch the things you gave your life to, broken,
And stoop and build them up with worn out tools:
If you can make one heap of all your winnings
And risk it on one turn of pitch and toss,
And lose and start again at your beginnings
And never breathe a word about your loss;
If you can force your heart and nerve and sinew
To serve your turn long after they are gone,
And so hold on when there is nothing in you
Except the Will which says to them: Hold on!
If you can talk with crowds and keep your virtue,
Or walk with Kings nor lose the common touch,
If neither foes nor loving friends can hurt you,
If all men count with you, but none too much;
you can wait and not be tired by waiting,
Or being lied about don't deal in lies,
Or being hated don't give way to hating,
If you can fill the unforgiving minute
With sixty seconds worth of distance run,
Yours is the Earth and everything that is in it,
And - which is more - you will be a Man, my son.

When he finished he did not say another word. The experience was so exceptional I cried.

Out loud, with my voice shaking, I said "How gifted you are… or is this a miracle in disguise?"

This poem defined the disturbances of mind, body and soul in my immediate future. This man had only a glimmer of existence contained within him. I am mystified; was his spirit speaking to me?

Isaac made me cry. It wasn't easy to start working again. On my first day back I asked Isaac what day it was.

"You don't even know what day it is? *I* wouldn't trust you with patients," he sarcastically replied.

I had very low confidence, especially with comments like that. How could it be any other way?

The day Isaac told me he wouldn't trust me with patients was an important one. At New Wellesley Hospital, a teaching hospital where I worked for six years, I learned how to intubate patients in the operating room under the guidance of an anesthesiologist.

Forty years ago only the doctors intubated patients, passing a tube into the lungs. It was a big responsibility. Quickness, accuracy and a steady hand were needed to pass the tube into the patients' lungs. Isaac couldn't shake my ability. I was confident now as I performed my duties as respiratory therapist.

There were no long maternity leaves at work. If you were fortunate you had two weeks off. Most mothers remained home but I preferred to work.

Eugene helped; he was sixteen and watched his three brothers. When I worked there were never any babysitters other than Eugene. I didn't trust anyone else, especially with my children. I knew the real world whereas Isaac was born with a silver spoon in his mouth. It was like we were from two different galaxies and didn't even speak the same language.

In 2001 I lost my job because of a psychotic episode caused by a shot of cortisone. My employer's idea of Workmen's Compensation was to give me two years of college free but under one condition: I had to pass their preliminary tests in math, English and other subjects.

I went to a memory clinic for testing at BMC because l also needed to have an IQ test. I remember the day well; the woman testing me must've been a therapist.

I'm not really sure what her title was, she just asked a lot of bizarre questions like, "Where does the sun set?" and "Where does the sun rise?"

I know this sounds strange but I had no idea as to the answers. After many questions she said, "Are you like this all the time?"

I think after that statement this woman was sure I wasn't going to college. She gave me an IQ of 80, only two points above mental retardation.

I always knew I would never work in a hospital again, no matter how stable I was, no doctor had to tell me that. I had an interview with a Dr. Pain to determine eligibility for Disability. "You can work again."

Who was insane, him or me?

My employers refused to give me the two years college that was promised me, so I went to Mass Rehab. This is where I met my caseworker, who was an angel. The only way I can describe her is, she never gave up on me. She did all the paperwork for me so I received a Pell grant and was able to take three classes. Although english and math were not up to college level, my reading was. I had to take basic writing. In my whole life I only wrote one sentence, never a real paper; how could I be expected to pass?

I had to take basic writing again. My son Andrew was responsible for my achieving this goal. He spent many hours helping me with math and English. I also had tutors from Williams College and Berkshire community college. My English teacher also helped me pass. When I took the final exam my professor said, "Take as long as you want to finish."

It took six hours but I passed. I was psychotic at the time and this was not an easy undertaking. But it has never been my nature to give up. After I passed the exam Jack, Andrew and I attended Berkshire Community College together. Isn't that odd, going to college with your children? Both boys were in there twenties and I was at least 50 at the time.

My children benefited too. Of course they had perfect attendance because I was going with them and being the responsible one, we were never late. At the end of the year the faculty gave a party for the ones with perfect attendance. I was on the honor roll at least three times and belonged to Phi Beta Kappa.

At that time I was receiving the best mental health care available in the Berkshires. My therapist of fifteen years couldn't believe that my IQ was 80. I guess I was getting better. She was the key to my sanity.

Andrew also tried to teach me how to sing. He used to tell me, "Sing louder! Belt it out!"

God, this was fun! We sang the song by John Denver, *"Take me home, country roads, to the place where I belong! West Virginia, mountain ma-ma, take me home, country roads."*

It's such irony because in 1972 his dad and I used to play that song over and over on the juke box down the street.

Now, let's end on a funny note. There was another patient, an Italian man in his late eighties, in the hospital. I asked him the same question I asked everyone: How did he get through hard times?

"FUCKA EVERYBODY YOU CAN!!!!" he replied with a hearty voice.

"Thank you, Mister Monty," I answered in a soft voice.

Today I am the last one alive in my first respiratory department.

PARANORMAL SPIRITUAL REALITY

One time while she was dancing at a bar, my sister Doris met a man from India whose father had taught him to read palms. He asked me if he could read mine. I told him he could and he did so with astonishing accuracy.

"You will have four sons and one I cannot see. You will remarry but the marriage won't last. You will have a major illness at thirty-seven, but you will recover. You will have a profession and some college, but you will not live to old age," he softly predicted.

The child he couldn't see referred to the abortion I had when I was in my twenties. The rest that he said came to pass, except that I would not live to old age.

My dad heard his prophecy and said, "You met the devil himself."

This sent shivers up my spine. When I had my breakdown I held on to what the palm reader said: *I would recover.*

My father was an atheist and didn't believe in the devil. My mother believed in a devil and in god. Dad had no belief system but when he was dying he asked me, "Susan, do you think there's an afterlife?"

"Yes, there is a nonphysical realm. I recognized and identified this unworldly terrain," I said in a convincing voice. Dad listened. He wasn't convinced but I put doubt in his mind. That much I could see from his expression.

Sometimes it seemed as though a spiritual warfare was going on in my life. I experienced different kinds of spiritual activity. My brain found other frequencies. In my altered state of mind, my brain was a radio that picked up numerous stations. Each station had its own genre—my realm of insanity, a spiritual realm, a realm of the dead, realms of trans-mind states, out-of-body experiences, inner-body experiences and demonic possession.

Once when I was in bed, I heard thunderous footsteps coming down the hallway. A faceless shadowed figure grabbed me and pulled me toward the wall, crossing my arms at the wrists. I froze and became frantic with fear; then it suddenly ended. I didn't understand the hallway; my apartment had no hallways. Maybe I was mistaken and it was vivid nightmare…or was it?

Seth and I never left the bed. It seemed we were attached at the hip, Siamese twin-style. One day as I looked down at him, his eyes changed; the right remained blue while the left turned green. Seconds later they reversed; the right eye became green and the left, blue. The colors changed back and forth several times before it stopped. I thought, *Wow!*

I had my first hallucination while having a cup of tea with Seth. As we sipped the tea I found myself in a daze, staring into his eyes. Suddenly his face became grotesque and started to melt. The more I looked, the more it melted. I was horrified and broke my gaze, screaming, "What was that?"

Seth said, "The eyes are the mirror to your soul."

He was severely psychotic at this time, though I did not know. I worried about what he'd said, that the eyes were the mirror to the soul. If that was true then my soul must be very ugly. Would I become another Dorian Gray? Would I stay young and be pretty forever, while my soul became uglier?

My second hallucination revealed three Native American faces hovering over Seth's head and looking into my eyes. They were very old with many wrinkles of time gone by and seemed full of wisdom. As I searched within their eyes, I felt a connection. Could it be my American Indian heritage? Were they trying to help me? Were they shamans showing me how to travel to other dimensions?

I believed I was a shaman and could restore people to perfect health. I don't know if I was delusional… or if this was an invitation to experience the new world surrounding me.

A third time, at an AA meeting, a man stood close to me…*Oh no, I can't believe it, another face is melting!* But when I turned my head, his face stopped melting. Suddenly time stood still. I looked around the room. For about a minute no one moved. This was more than disturbing; I worried, *What is happening to me?* I could move; why couldn't they? As quickly as it started, it stopped. Everything went back to normal, but for only a brief moment, then back to madness.

At another AA meeting, I saw clear through my arm to the table beneath. There was no flesh from my wrist to my elbow. I became terrified and mumbled,

"Oh, my God, I can see through my arm!"

No one heard me and if they did they'd think I was hallucinating. That was scary to me; this disclosure could give them another reason to shun me.

Suddenly the vision vanished, leaving me feeling I must have x-ray eyes.

I can't remember the hallucinations that I generated myself. Yet I can recollect the visions I did not control. There are, after all, people who are not crazy yet have outer body experiences more profound than mine. There are books but I find my experiences have been intertwined with other unique realities.

There was a time when I started seeing hallucinations more frequently. After a while I could create them at will. I wasn't afraid anymore. Yet while at the time these were exciting and pleasurable occurrences, in actuality I was getting deeper into the disorder. This domain was so touchable that actual reality seemed unreal, compared to my other world.

Some years ago, three months after my psychotic break in1989, I was invited to a born-again Christian service. Everyone went to the altar so I followed. Eve, the Sunday school teacher, tapped me on the shoulder. She said, "Come, I want to show you something you need to know."

We went to one of the pews. She opened the bible and read a verse: *If you follow me I will lead you through the wilderness and out the other side.* The implication was if I followed God's will and not mine, I would go from madness to sanity. I couldn't be an angel. Eve took this into consideration and remained at my side.

My AA sponsor Todd wanted to meet Eve. At the meeting she saw cobras wrapped around our necks. Although Todd was quite sane, he saw them too. What was this all about?

Snakes around the neck . . . similar to the snakes around my legs in my childhood . . . it is hard to believe both Todd and Eve saw them and neither knew the other. In Hinduism there isn't a temple or statue without a snake about his neck, as the Hindus believe in Lord Shiva.

Myths say snakes represent control of dark forces and temptation. They also signify the power of *kundalini,* the life energy. *Kundalini* is a spiritual transformation with many signs and symptoms resembling a psychotic breakdown. That's why people from the east feel it's essential for westerners to have an understanding of these spiritual phenomena.

The event with the snakes left me confused; it was scary. How could Todd and Eve see the same thing? What was the meaning? I may find the rational reason but I doubt it. Possibly the answer remains in a place at the end of a rainbow.

Three months after I left the hospital in 1989 Eve called me. "I have a significant message that affects your wellbeing. I have a suggestion for you and I will call you back," she said in a trembling voice.

I was curious as to the meaning. Was she all right? We had walked on some unholy ground together.

When I called Eve back she said, "I opened this manuscript and saw three Indian faces. One was called Shiva, the god of death and rebirth. Beware of a man that carries a sword. He is a dangerous man. He walks with a woman that has four children. I'm frightened!"

Maybe I should have been frightened, too… I was the one with four children.

"I was thrown from my bed and onto the floor the night after I read this. Whatever is pursuing you, it can't be good," Eve said to me.

Later I was sleeping in Jude's room when she was dying. One night my body was raised from the bed and hurled across the room, even more violently than Eve's experience. I hit the phone on the other side of the room. I prayed, *God with your wisdom, compassion, understanding, forgiveness, take my Jude in your arms and give her peace.*

It happened so fast I wasn't hurt, but it shook me up, leaving vibrations of terror within me. I thought about Eve and how startled and frightened she had been.

Was I in the presence of evil or was evil present inside of me. . . or both?

After Eve's experience she stopped calling. Was something chasing her? When I remember her warning, I think about Seth. In his psychotic state of mind, which was most of the time, he liked to portray himself as a Samurai swordsman. It looked like Eve meant Seth.

She was accurate; Seth was a dangerous person and unreasonable most of the time. Thank god he didn't have a real sword!

I had many out-of-body experiences; they started during meditation.

One was very peaceful, looking up through the trees at the sky. It was repeated three times. Another time I saw myself in my nightshirt in a meadow, while a large bird whirled about, almost hitting me. I got scared, moved and reentered my body.

At times I was on the ceiling looking down at my room, which is a very common meditation experience. Sometimes the ceiling opened up. The sky, moon and stars were visible. If I left would I get back? Scared, I moved and went back into my body again and I was looking into a candle flame. A golden person materialized—first the head, then the body. I saw no face but only two red eyes. How scary was this? Mighty scary! I must have moved as fast as a cheetah to stop that one.

The figure gradually disappeared. This always happened; my way back was just to move. Sometimes I wish I had let that vision finish so I could see what would have transpired.

Another time I was hovering, like a helicopter, above a camp fire with clusters of Stone Age people bunched around it. I only had a hurried glimpse of this when another vision appeared. Stark-naked human figures packed together crawled over each other. It was upsetting—a vision resembling Dante's hellish painting. The room became unbearably hot, almost to suffocation. It was one of my most frightening outer-body experience to date.

The paranormal was a large part of my life. I had experienced primordial noises, like screams, during sex for at least ten years. In 1997, my partner said, "Quiet, the neighbors will overhear us."

In the year 2000 things began to change. Along with the usual groans and growling like a mad dog in the middle of sex, a voice bellowed, new and violent in nature. I wasn't aware of this until my partner said, "A demonic, furious man's voice was communicating and it was coming from you."

I did not understand what he was speaking about, but at this point, I began to clench my teeth, thrash and pull off the sheets during sex. I was frightened. What was happening? How to end these hideous events?

Reiki was popular then, energy healing as an alternative to medicine. I made an appointment with a reiki master at a reiki treatment clinic in Vermont. The reiki teacher said, "Lie on the table and get relaxed and be comfortable."

Using her hands, she swept in a brushing motion above and across my head. In an instant I left my body. I could not see, but I could hear what was happening about me and within me.

Suddenly a heavy force produced an immeasurable pressure in my pelvis and curved my back skyward. My head and neck bowed like a branch in the wind; my mouth flew open and my jaw locked into position. Out came the voice of an angry man trapped in a hollow vessel. His speech was intensely angry with foul language. It was ear piercing and lasted quite some time then stopped. Simultaneously, multiple voices in different languages echoed and bounced off the walls like ping pong balls. Five students heard more loud voices coming from the room. What was going on?

A student behind the practitioner asked the man within me questions. He answered angrily and loudly enough to rupture my ear drums. I can't remember what he said, but the voices left. I went back to my body and sat up. The reiki master asked me what the spirits wanted. I said, "I think they wanted to be heard after being locked in me for who knows how long, maybe the beginning of time."

I suddenly felt at peace. A student asked the reiki master what made the spirits leave. In a confident voice she said, "We are healers. I saw angels in the corner of the room."

After this treatment the voices were gone, never to return. All the odd sexual conduct ceased. No more discomfort on my organ of utmost pleasure. No more grasping at the sheets. I was free of the voices that tormented me, but that was not the end.

Similar events still nipped at my heels. The reiki master sent me a letter with a number to call in an emergency. This number was a spiritual emergency number for people like me. *Wow!* I thought.

The reiki master thought I was having a kundalini awakening experience. She said I was tapping into the astral plane, where there could be hostile spirits in a dangerous atmosphere. She wrote a letter suggesting I discontinue my hazardous behavior. She felt obligated to give me this information. But I enjoyed it and didn't heed her warning.

I looked up the reiki master when writing this chapter in 2013. I asked her if she remembered my experience. She said, "It's too long ago."

When I tried to give her more information, she interrupted and said harshly, "Again, I'm not into that anymore."

I asked if she could put me in contact with one of the other ladies. She brushed me off, repeating that she didn't do this any longer.

I think I gave her a good scare that day. No one in that room could have forgotten what took place. The people in the hallway waiting for their appointments looked white, as if they'd seen a ghost putting fingers together like a cross. They were speechless.

The reiki teacher didn't want to get involved. She had a brush with the supernatural and I don't blame her for not wanting to come forward and corroborate my tale. I hope a student may read this book and comes forward to tell what really happened that day.

Trans-mind states began in 2007, when I connected with the astral plane. My trans-mind states are unearthly; a detached floating of my mind.

One afternoon Andrew and I were sitting on the couch talking about a woman and man that had died nearby. As I talked coldness encircled our feet along with a feeling of nonbeing. Andrew became uneasy and then frightened.

Now he saw this actually happening; it wasn't a parlor trick. People talked through me as my lips moved and sounds came forth. They were not bad-tempered people like before. I sang in a woman's operatic voice, although I can't sing a note. Andrew asked me to stop. Once the singing ceased, the coldness about his ankles dissipated and things went back to normal. He never doubted me again.

It was very easy to go into trans-mind states. The operatic high-pitched sounds and native Indian chanting tones were the most common states.

An experience happened in the pool. I wasn't a good swimmer but when I entered the water I swam rapidly, without stopping, for thirty minutes. I didn't possess that kind of cardiovascular endurance, yet the energy was immense, as though another being was within me. After swimming I babbled in a low voice in another dialect. I thought, *What the hell is transpiring? Should I stop? What might emerge?* Something unholy… But I was curious. Curiosity might kill this cat… and satisfaction might not bring me back.

One day as I sat on the sofa, two hands encircled my head, covering my ears. A woman said in a tender tone of voice, "I'm a shaman and I will show a marvelous spectacle that borders on disbelief."

I was unable to release her firm grip. Usually moving broke the trance but in this case, I could not break it, no matter how hard I tried. She said, "We will travel through the cosmos."

I wanted no part of this but I had no way to halt it.

I saw huge pink worm-holes extending past comprehension of time. I felt like I was sliding down a laundry chute at tremendous speed, unable to escape the woman's grip. I never experienced a journey like this, an invitation to go further than the beyond. I enjoyed the voyage. During my madness there were hallucinations but this wasn't one. This was so real, it was spooky. *What the hell...?*

Was I on a whole new plane in the universe or were the pits of hell raining chaos in my mind? Possibly both. What a trip!

A tunnel was a common vision when I meditated. It was pitch-black and with a light at the end. I was fully conscious but only once was able to reach the light and it encircled me. Sometimes people walked slowly with me, but most of the time I was unaccompanied in this meeting place between the physical and spiritual realms.

Often I would lie down in my bed and gaze at a candle flame as it flickered. One time the flame suddenly opened like a flower and became a ball of fire that intensified until my two eyes became one, like a telescope in the middle of my forehead. As I approached visions such as this, I forced myself to come back.

Seth also experienced this world and still does. He scares me when he sees huge spiders crawling up his apartment building; I was always frightened of spiders.

Seth told me people came at night to have sex with him. Was he crazy or was he truly having sex with other people? He swore that it was of a ghostly nature.

I thought he was crazier than I originally thought until I was in bed alone one night. I felt a soft supple hand reach between my legs to my sexual opening then gently retreat. So it appears Seth wasn't as crazy as I thought. An unearthly thing was happening to me and I realized we both shared this connection.

In 1998, an inner-body experience happened during sex. My sexual organs became painful even when stroked softly. When the pain became extreme, the inner body experience occurred. I went inside myself and then far away. It was not an out-of-body experience of floating above my body, seeing myself in the bed.

My boyfriend Bob and I were making love and I was experiencing a climax that was so on fire and would not stop it was terrifying! I lost myself and found myself floating in a dark space, a universe without stars. It felt so peaceful I wanted to stay there, but then I got scared. *Could this be insanity? I must get back to my body!* In a flash I was back.

I started talking in a childlike voice and said, "Bob, please, can we do this again?"

"Are you crazy? We've been making love for three hours."

He had never experienced anything quite like this and said in an elated voice, "Any man would pay $1,000 to have slept with you tonight!" Then he slapped a quarter on my ass.

Bob never explained what he understood about that night and what took place… but it must've been pretty good to pay $1,000.

I explained this to my therapist. She said, "And when you came back you talked like a little child."

How did she know this? Did someone else have the same experience?

The therapist told me not to play with my mind. I was convinced this was a divine involvement with the womb of the universe, where birth takes place. I discovered how to get there. I could bring myself to the brink but not enter, just be close to this place, knowing if I opened the door only peace awaited me. But one time wasn't enough and I understood that it was not my time to stay.

When I went to college and said farewell to that gruesome universe. I put the reiki aside and no longer had time to create my scary little world. Entering school, studying hard and doing homework kept me from thinking about these planes of reality. Everyone wants to believe in magic, but this magic wasn't a cute little fairy tale; it was the risky opposite.

To this day, the thought always comes back that my experiences were real. When speaking of such things to someone without mental illness, they think I am still crazy. But if I speak to someone who has mental illness, they understand me completely and also may have had scary moments like mine. Most people are reluctant to share stories like these, afraid of rejection.

My son Jack experienced a paranormal experience in his bedroom. He felt a force, like a thud, enter him. His explanation was similar to mine when I first started deep meditation. Through his closed eyes, he saw an apparition of a girl, all in white and as big as him. He was spellbound as she grabbed his shoulders and they hovered about the ceiling, then moved to a distant corner of the room, where she placed him in his bed.

I asked him what she wanted. Jack said, his voice still shaking, "I think she wanted to show me something, but what, I do not know." Jack doesn't like to talk about this experience.

I began talking with a woman that had BPD about the experiences I spoke of in this chapter. When we finished, it was evident that there were people who could understand this episode. I can speak their language and we're no longer alone!

I believe that with mental illness there occur hallucinations, but also visions of a spiritual realm. Hallucinations are not real and I know this. But sometimes it wasn't a chemical imbalance, or symptom of a mental illness. My illness allowed me to visit different spiritual realms, good and evil. Having experienced this world, I want to go back, to discern which reality is real. But the fear of getting stuck there is unthinkable.

Hallucinations and out-of-body experiences were not the only thing that affected me. I also had premonitions, always of someone close to me dying. Two premonitions—one of a doctor and one of a coworker— stand out in my mind. Both times I had identical nightly premonitions that I couldn't stop.

The first forewarning came in 1987, two years before my psychotic break. I wasn't crazy then. I dreamed of the death of Shawn Gates, a doctor who I felt a fondness toward and respected.

I began to wake up every night covered in sweat, haunted by the vision of a man killed on a motorcycle. I couldn't see his face and his back was to me. All my premonitions were similar in this way—only the back showed; their identity was never exposed.

I soon found all my premonitions were meticulously correct in their nature, with the utmost horrifying feature that person's demise. It was always someone I cared about, who also cared about me. I was petrified that the man I saw could be Eugene, who was living in Orlando, Florida and owned a candy red motorcycle.

Dr. Shawn Gates was a plastic surgeon in his early forties and one of the most sought-after bachelors in Boston. I was thirty-four when I met him and had just delivered twin boys. The skin on my abdomen hung in folds and exercise couldn't repair it. This didn't fit the rest of me; I felt like I had a deformity and decided to change it. I had a tummy tuck. I was physically fit and strong, not a pinch of fat on my body. I could defeat men in tennis, not only because I was a quick thinker, but because of my physical wellbeing.

On my first visit Doctor Gates and I sat across from each other at a small table. Shawn leaned over and kissed me on the lips ever so gently. The kiss said, "I like you." Unfortunately, this would be a short-lived relationship between us. So sad; never will I forget him and his warm, giving nature.

Because I was in the medical field, Doctor Gates gave me professional courtesy and lowered his fee to make the surgery possible. We went to a small room with a surgical table. Doctor Gates sat on the table and took a large quantity of nude "before" photos.

My yard was an old dumping place in the 1800s. I found ink wells, clay jugs and whiskey flasks, as well as a lot of clay pipes. The pipes I found were manmade and mass-produced and broken at the stem. Timothy DeWitt's clay pipes made him a wealthy man. Since there was a lot of tuberculosis, if you wanted a smoke the owner broke off a small piece from the stem. That way you could take a puff and the owner could snap off the piece your lips were on.

I was in the habit of digging up old bottles. Some bottles were embossed with words, like "Kickapoo Indian Oil." All were different colors and shapes; many were blue. For me, digging was like rummaging in pursuit of treasure. Finding the origin was often more fun than finding a particular piece. I took each bottle, washed and cleaned it, then brought it to the library to see what it was used for.

Dr. Gates soon moved his practice to Beverly Hills, California. I missed him.

When Doctor Gates told me he was leaving, I gave him a special bottle I'd found, for his office in California. "Protector" was engraved in big letters on the front of the bottle. I filled it with sweet-smelling dried flower petals and put a dried rose on the cover. Later he placed it in his home. This made me feel meaningful. It was my first offering to a doctor and he put it in a special place.

This behavior of giving bottles to doctors, then life sculptures and artwork, was my peace offering at my journey's end. I was edgy, with restless feelings about the past. I was unknowingly healing myself from the past memories of that damaging doctor in my youth.

Before Doctor Gates left, he took out his prescription pad and wrote down the number where I could reach him at any time. He said, "If you need me: anything whatsoever, Susan and I mean it: never forget me. If you come to California I'll show you around."

What a special invitation this was! This offer made me feel exceptional although the understanding was friendship. This made my head spin in a good way, in a way I never felt before. But I was married at the time and knew this was impossible. My husband would never agree to such a thing.

Some time passed and I received a letter from Dr. Gates. He asked about my bottle digging and mentioned missing Boston in fall, the bright reds and yellows of the leaves and perfect weather in September. He said his dog had bumped the bottle I gave him with his tail; the rose cap survived but the bottle was completely in pieces. He wrote, *Are you still digging? I would love a second bottle in place of the fragmented one.*

After reading this letter, I positioned it in my massive family bible, which dates back to 1827. It had countless pages, which would make the letter almost impossible to locate.

One day, after another night of waking in cold sweats, seeing the man on the motorcycle, I felt the need to write to Doctor Gates. I wrote a short note for his birthday and signed it *Sincerely, Susan.* I wanted to put *Love, Susan* but I was married and found it too personal.

Something in my gut said to stop at the post office instead of my mail box. Later I would understand why I chose this speedier method. All of these actions appeared quite unusual and played a large part in the happenings that would be clarified in the upcoming events.

One evening while I was working, a nurse I knew approached me. "You know Dr. Gates?" she asked.

"Yes," I said.

"He's been killed in a motorcycle accident on Ventura Highway in California."

I became hysterical. Although I was absorbed with this update I was determined to complete my rounds, as I had a substantial amount of patients that evening. Even though my boss said I could go home, I stayed. I had the ability to shut down my emotions and managed to complete the shift. But I needed answers about his death and the events preceding, so I could have closure.

The next day I called his office and spoke with Sally, his original secretary from Boston. "Did he get my letter?" I asked.

She said, "He received your letter and he made some notations."

His main secretary had the same news. "He jotted down some notes," she sniffled.

I was so upset, I didn't ask what it said. She described how he was killed. It had just started to rain that night and the highway was slippery, covered in a slick, greasy film. As a result, his bike slid crossways. The bones and vertebrae connecting his spinal cord to his neck snapped and shattered.

I was astonished he'd even had a motorcycle and took a chance of harming his valuable hands. Those competent hands had corrected disfigurements and make people look fine again. He was too young to die, with such a promising future ahead of him. His compassion and kindness helped many people feel better about themselves. Never will I forget him and his warm, giving nature. I had lost the most genuine and caring person. He liked me, and so I felt like I was a real person, not silly, or unpleasant to look at.

I went to my family bible for his letter. Because there were no records of marriages, births and deaths kept at city halls, people used the bible to record these events. I frantically looked through the bible searching for the letter. As luck would have it (or was it luck?) the letter was in the section on births, marriages and deaths. Was this odd placement of the letter a coincidence?

After Doctor Gates' death the premonitions stopped. A few weeks later everyone knew he had died. I was working in the ER and overheard a doctor say "Sometimes you have to stop and smell the roses."

He was accurate with that statement. Today I have planted thirteen rose bushes. All the roses are in different colors and I smell them every day. And when they die I collect their petals and put them in a special place.

In 1992 I worked in a nursing facility in Providence, Rhode Island. I was the underdog. The nurses on the night shift wanted me fired. People like that have to find someone to taunt. They picked me and a man named Karl and discriminated against us to the extreme.

Karl was a perceptive thirty-year-old man with two strikes against him: he was black and he was gay. I was discriminated against because I was mentally ill, with no voice and vulnerable to everyone.

When the nurses were scheming, Karl hid in the closet and eavesdropped on their strategies. He said, "Susan, they're looking for inaccuracies in your charting, to get you fired."

I said, "Karl, thank you for the warning."

His snooping didn't change the outcome. My notes were accurate and I had a Massachusetts license as a respiratory therapist. However, I was psychotic and on Stellazine and the requirements for a license in Rhode Island were different. My Massachusetts license requirements were inadequate so I was let go. The nurse, a loathsome person, got her way.

I only heard from Karl once. "Hairdressing is my job now and I love it," he said. He seemed quite happy. This was our last conversation.

It was some time later, in the summer, that the nightmares began. At three o'clock in the morning, I would wake up, crying hysterically. The tears wouldn't diminish; I had to go out and drive until I stopped crying. The night air was so pleasant and soothing it helped me to relax. It was only then that I could drive home and sleep.

The premonition happened nightly and continued for months; it was relentless. A man faced away from me, a repeating occurrence in my premonitions. I saw a bed and a shadowed figure on the floor. Men with clubs were breaking down the door. Glass shattered from the window above the bed. What did this all mean? Of course I could only speculate; I didn't have a crystal ball.

Betty, my nurse friend, called. She said, "Susan, did you hear about Karl? He overdosed on pills."

I received more information; he may have changed his mind and wanted to live. He was trying to reach the phone to get help and fell to the floor. The police knocked down the door and found him lying there.

Betty and I agreed: my repeated dream was of Karl's suicide. He didn't make it to the phone and fell to the floor. The shadow lying on the floor wasn't a shadow; it was Karl. The smashing glass was his spirit leaving his body.

In the movie *The Sixth Sense,* the dead wanted a boy to complete the unfinished business they had before dying. I related to this movie. Although people didn't come to me physically, what was familiar was their requests.

I no longer woke up crying at three o'clock in the morning. I thought back to my job and how the nurses antagonized Karl. His partner left him and Karl was unable to handle this sorrow. He took his life because he couldn't see any way out. I realized what he wanted of me. I had to call O'Leary, the nurse who was the main attacker. I was sure she would relay my message to her comrades.

I called her and said, "O'Leary, you may have killed one spirit, but you won't kill mine."

O'Leary said, "Who is this?"

I'm certain she knew as I hung the phone up. After I finished Karl's unfinished business I never woke up crying at three o'clock again.

I had the most delightful, brilliant counselor during my numerous admissions to the psychiatric unit. John was beyond a therapist; this was just his title. He was a friend to everyone and everyone loved him; everyone was his equal. If there was perfection he owned it. John had dark hair, dark eyes and olive colored skin. He spoke many languages; his personality was gentle and sympathetic. When my sons were there he would play chess with them. He listened to my every word.

John was always smiling. Soon his smiles left as he went through a bitter divorce, though I wasn't aware this was happening.

A year after I was hospitalized, my son Michael, asked, "Mom, did you hear about John? He shot himself." At first I thought it was someone else. Michael described him; it was indeed John.

Why did John take his life? He had information, tools, coping skills... and yet he was unable to ask for comfort and support. He continually provided support to others, always knowing exactly what to say and do. John had many friends well-trained in the mental health field, to reassure him and ease him through his dark days with encouragement and most important, love.

John's depression was so bad he had no ladder left to climb; the rungs were breaking, making it impossible to reach the top: sunshine, happiness and most of all relief from the non-stop anguish and grief connected to his divorce. Depression uses brutal sledgehammers on the soul, not allowing remission. To fight back alone can be a losing battle.

Yes. He lost.

John used to tell me that I wore my heart on my sleeve. One day after he walked me to my car he said, "I'm not afraid of crazy." Of course he meant me. Another time he kissed me in the nurses' station, a friendly kiss that made me feel special.

I think when John's marriage was in despair he was reaching out to someone who identified with his pain... me. When it came to pain I was a professional. I knew this foe and how to outthink it, though I was not always successful.

John asked me to call him when I returned from my vacation. He was very interested in me; I wasn't sure if it was a relationship he wanted. I sent him a short note when I returned from my holiday.

I discussed our relationship with my therapist and asked if I should respond. She said, "He'll only try to fix you."

I was not his equal.

On this advice, I left it alone. There are times when I think about it. Had I returned his friendliness, would it have changed the outcome? I will never know the answer. If I have regrets, this is one of them.

After his death I was meditating; a figure in a grey mist slowly came towards me. First the nose appeared, then the eyes and last the face. The figure had a dusky complexion, with dark hair and dark eyes.

I knew immediately that it was my dear friend John. He came near so I would not be mistaken, gazed upon me and then gradually turned, walking back into the grayish fog. I've always questioned where this dwelling was, this cloudy, hazy terrain. Could this be where suicide victims go, not seeing what is in front of them, encircled in gloomy smog?

P'TA: The Love of My Life

Personal & Private Collection of Susan Rose   The Williamstown Hobo

When I first met Peter I told myself that could be me, homeless like years ago after my psychotic break.

If I lost my medical insurance, where would I get money for my medication? Just one costs $1,000, never mind the other eight. This was an excruciating thought indeed. I could be back on the streets with no one to help me. People would look through me as if I were invisible. My behavior and exterior would scare any sane person away; there would be no longer be a helping hand to get me support and stop this horrifying state of mind, body and spirit. This thought stayed only a moment as I fixed my eyes on Peter.

There was something behind that rough exterior shining through and the peace in his eyes was remarkable. Now that ten years have passed I have come to believe something more was in Peter's eyes. His childlike innocence was what I craved and what drew me to him. It destroyed that which was taken by force *Thank you, Peter, for taking my hand and leading me to the peaceful place within; I am no more the wounded child. My love, you set me free. God bless.*

With Love,

Susan.

When I met Peter Mitchell in Williamstown, he was pushing a bicycle with garbage bags attached and flags everywhere, probably so cars could see him. In the bags were redeemable cans. I was taking a course in photography at Berkshire Community College. I thought his homelessness would be a thought-provoking theme for my photography class.

In this Ivy League College town, he stuck out like a sore thumb. He was quite a spectacle and *Whiff!* His bike, which he affectionately called Granny, was more like Frankenstein. Every piece was from a different bicycle. He carried patch kits for flats.

The first time I saw him, his bicycle was propped up against a tree. He was carrying a radio and a bag of batteries that he found on the roadside. I was in my car driving around and around the rotary trying to get the guts to approach him. I said to myself, "He can only say no and I can accept that."

I parked my car and walked up to him. I excitedly asked, "May I take your photograph, sir?"

With a toothless grin he said, "Sure ma'am."

Peter had a distinctive stink of rubbish and body odor. I didn't want to get too near. The stench was overwhelming but then in a sweet voice he said, "Give me a hug." How could I say no? I just held my breath.

Peter's hands were black as coal. He wore black jeans covered with food spots here and there. With his shirt that had only one button and a baseball cap with the American flag on it, he resembled a famous half-painted canvas, spills of paint in different colors everywhere. Flags were attached to his bicycle as warning signs so cars could see him, not because he was patriotic. It was quite the opposite. He told me how the Army tortured him.

I took twelve photographs of him. He seemed to be a happy fellow. Unlike a regular bum, he had a plan. Peter never stayed in one place for long. He pulled out a map and revealed the trip he was planning. With his toothless smile he told me, "I'm on my way to Oregon."

With a smile I stressed, "Let's keep in touch," and gave him my phone number.

He had only had thirteen cents on him at the time, enough for nothing. I told him, "When you get to Oregon call me collect."

I was 54 years old, while he was 57. He was very charismatic and I never saw so much peace in someone's eyes. Could it be his heart shining through those beautiful blue eyes? It was hard to see through Peter's exterior but something told me he was more than special. He had the spirit of an angel.

I never thought I would see him again. But he stayed long enough for us to have our first date in a park directly across from Williamstown's library. We had a picnic. I brought strawberries, cold cuts and cheese. He brought something too; it looked familiar.

I asked with surprise, "Is it sumac?"

He replied, "The birds eat it. Taste; it's like berries."

Reluctantly I gave it just a little nibble. Later I found out that if it had leaves that pointed down it was poison sumac; thank god it was the one with leaves that pointed up! Stupid me, cows eat grass, so should I eat grass, too? I was getting sucked into this man's reality, or more likely, psychosis.

Peter had difficulty eating the food I brought, because he had no teeth. He would take small bites and gum it to death. His gums were hard as nails like his feet, tough-skinned because he walked so much.

After we ate, Peter started rolling around the grass and on the blanket like a little kid, quoting the Bible. I wasn't that familiar with the Bible; he spoke of an ass that talked and told me he believed in interspecies communication.

He burst out, "Susan, I think I love you."

I was shocked. I didn't know what to say, so I said nothing. I asked, "May I tape-record our conversation?"

It was a great day to get our conversation on tape; I would have something to remember him by. As he was leaving he said, "Let's see who wins the fun contest today! I bet I will."

I said, "Sure, why not!"

His eyes, always so peaceful, shone like beacons of happiness. I had captured them in black and white photos with my 35-mm camera. The paper and chemicals were expensive but that didn't stop me from taking lots of pictures of Peter before he left for Oregon that day.

I thought I would never see him again. I was quite sure he wouldn't call. I was stunned when he did. I was in the North Adams Regional Hospital psychiatric ward; my son Jack relayed the message.

He said, "He just wants to talk to you, that's all."

Peter didn't know that I was in the hospital; Jack didn't know Peter and said I was on vacation. The strangest thing was that I was admitted after our picnic lunch. I was having a severe panic attack with increasing hypomania; I needed hospitalization. I told the therapist all about me meeting this hobo.

He said in a surprised voice, "I know who you're talking about. His name is Peter and he slept on my back porch last night."

I told him I took a bit of the sumac. He explained that one was poison. He asked very seriously, "You sure you want to be admitted… or have some more Peter fun-time?"

But my meeting with Peter had put me into a heightened state of mind. Learning about the sumac didn't help matters any; could I be poisoned? Who was this strange fellow and would he be back?

I went to a Jewish religious service scheduled at 2:00 PM on the ward. A Rabbi came.

I spoke about this hobo I had contact with.

He said, "Let him go."

But I didn't heed his words and now I am surely glad I didn't take his advice.

School began the day before I was released from the hospital. I was shaky but I attended class; my dad instilled responsibility in me at an early age. I said timidly to my photography professor, "I was just discharged yesterday from the psychiatric ward called the Greylock Pavilion at North Adams Regional Hospital; I'm a little shaky today but next week I'll be fine."

We were learning to develop film in a darkroom. This was difficult for me and at first I needed help. It took longer for me to accomplish the assignments than the younger students. Professor Williams was patient and kind to me; we keep in contact even today.

When I went to photography class, everyone always asked, "What photos do you have for us today, Susan?" They loved the photos I took of Peter. I even submitted two photos for publication in the 'Zine, a small book of poems and photographs. One picture was of Peter under a bridge.

I knew Peter was walking to Oregon, with plans to stop in New York City to commemorate 9/11. So I was surprised when two months later I saw a man pushing a bike by the roadside… and realized it was Peter. I stopped and stared.

Peter sweetly said to me, "Susan, I walked as far as Syracuse and then your charm, like an enormous rubber band, pulled me back to North Adams."

I blurted out, "I love you."

When I returned home, I threw the door to my car open as I announced to everyone, "I'm in love with a hobo."

I was impressed by Peter's determination, walking that distance to see me again. He only wanted to know if I received his letters.

Peter wandered south for a while, then east, all to see if he could get another hug from me. He said with vigor, "Can you imagine that there is a guy in this world who would walk thousands of miles to get a hug from you? You, dear Susan, are important to me. I've been doing some excellent writing while under your spell. I've been trying to write these stories for thirty years; so maybe you can understand why you're so important and I will try to show you. Symbiotic relations Ommmmmm-music! Someday Susan, I will be saying goodbye, waving my hand as I walk offstage saying, 'Susan have a good life'."

Did he know what the future would hold? He came close.

Our relationship began only two years after my psychotic break. Those two years I had spent sitting on my couch staring at the wall. How sad was that? It was an enormous waste of time. I was experiencing agoraphobia in addition to my bipolar disorder and psychosis. I woke up at six o'clock in the morning with extreme anxiety. I would get my mail but would not dare step into the street. My therapist gave me a book about dealing with worry and said, "When you wake, get up."

I took her advice and my anxiety started to diminish, but I still sat staring at the wall. I made up for it ten times over by enthusiastically living to the fullest, thanks to Peter.

Peter became my magic potion; he called me the medicine lady. I was still very vulnerable and this made it easy to get sucked into his reality, a fantasy world he created and lived in for 26 years while crisscrossing the country. I must say learning about his lifestyle was romantic at the time. My life was shifting. No more couch-sitting and Peter was responsible. One of the things we did daily was get up at 5:00 AM and check the trash cans for redeemable containers.

I was having fun checking the trash cans until my son Jack said, in a nasty voice, "I heard from a friend that you are picking up cans in the trash! Mom, that is embarrassing. If you need the money I will give you some. There are bags of dog shit in those trash cans."

I had plenty of money and Jack's words didn't bother me; I was having fun. One time Peter and I discovered in the college dumpster wine, in a box with a spout. We decided to have a drink... but of course Peter drank most of it. Another time we found a Dunkin' Donuts box full of munchkin doughnuts and a box of coffee with a spout. We had a feast. I was getting a taste of Peter's lifestyle. Peter had become my panacea and I his goddess.

One day at dusk I met Peter down near the bridge in Williamstown. In a loud voice he said, "Let's run and scream!"

We did just that. This was something a little child might do and Peter was childlike. Yet, I found him to be very charismatic. We went to the river bank and watched the beavers swim, then enjoyed looking at a horse farm on the other side of the river. A donkey voice echoed across the waterway. The only noise was the sounds of nature. Peter used to say, "Make music not noise, MMMMMMMMMM and friends not enemies."

We wrote a poem together about running by the tracks that night, running and screaming like little children.

"I go through town invisibly," he said.

I knew what he meant; that was just on my mind.

He said with elation, "I walk everywhere and prayer works! The sky is my wallpaper."

I thought, *What a unique way to describe this sky.*

He also said, "I call myself moving water!"

That seemed an appropriate name for a man who never stood still, moving state to state, like a stream rushing down the mountainside.

One night we slept near the river in a sleeping bag. Never in my entire life had I slept outside, in the pitch-black. It was definitely a new experience. The unforeseen was intimidating. Would there be animals? People that might harm me? The unexpected made me uncomfortable but I reminded myself, *Peter will know what to do. He loves me. He would give his life for me.* I knew this; he didn't have to tell me. Being with him reduced my fear to an acceptable level. I never even heard the train pass twenty yards from where I was sleeping; it didn't wake me up.

One day we were walking down the street of an upper class area when Peter noticed a tree fort on someone's property. In a cheerful voice, he said, "Let's climb it!"

I was reluctant at first because this was someone else's property, but Peter talked me into it. Acting like a kid was quite fun. After a while I forgot we were on someone else's property. No one noticed we played there for so long. I was having the time of my life.

After a short period of time Peter came to live with me but not in the house; his first bed was on my front porch. "I don't want to get soft," he said.

Gradually, Peter began to sleep on the floor in my house. It was a slow process and painful to his psyche. In the winter, the heat in the house was too warm for him. He would say, "What are you doing, trying to cook me?"

His body actually radiated heat. I was always cold. On my birthday he bought me a hot water bottle and filled it with hot water. This increased my body temperature and made it easier for me to get to sleep.

Peter and I hiked up Mount Greylock, the largest mountain in the state of Massachusetts. The destination was Peck's Falls, a popular place on the trail with a beautiful waterfall and tranquil basin. There was a lean-to for shelter and a fire pit for cooking.

Costello, my gentle-mannered German shepherd, came along for the adventure. All we had was Costello's bowl and Peter insisted on using it to cook our food. He said, "The fire will sterilize it."

So I ate out of the dog's dish. What choice did I have?

We spent four days there… in the rain. I was very uncomfortable because I never went camping and after this, I was convinced I'd never want to go again. Peter was mad because I forgot my sleeping bag and had to use his.

There was no water other than the stream that came from the mountains. Peter was used to drinking this water but I wasn't. He convinced me to drink the water. I didn't realize deer and other animals pooped in the water and I got quite severe diarrhea. I couldn't wait to get out of there.

I wanted to strangle him when he left me there and went back to get supplies. It was 2:00AM and no Peter. By this time I was scared. *He may not return and I may have to find my way down myself!* I tried to get warm by snuggling up to Costello, who looked at me in a strange way; maybe he was thinking, *What does she think she's doing?*

Peter finally reached the campsite and told me what happened. It turned out he had made a wrong turn; it was dark and he missed the trail. He went halfway down the other side of the mountain before he realized it. It was starting to get chilly.

I was still scared and mad both at the same time. There was no sexual encounter.

One time when we were in a church parking lot, he gently touched my ear lobe. I felt a wonderful sensation and thought to myself, *Maybe there could be more to this relationship.* I never knew such a soft gentle touch, just like I did way back as a little girl at the fifth grade dance, thinking, *I'd like to get some more.*

Then Peter kissed me and I couldn't wait to get home to brush my teeth. He was so dirty, I thought I might get something. The next day at my dentist appointment, I asked if it was possible to catch something from him. She said no and handed me an extra tooth brush and toothpaste. She had no idea he was toothless.

However, after a while his lack of hygiene didn't matter. I was falling in love with a bona fide vagabond. Twenty years ago a multimillionaire wanted to marry me but I said no. I didn't love him. How ironic that all my life I was looking for love, but was incapable of giving or receiving affection of any kind until now. I had fallen in love with a man who had only a penny in his pocket. The next ten years with him would teach me the importance of loving and being loved. It was the medicine that played a better part in healing the past and present and caused my recovery from a crippling mental illness. If love wasn't a cure-all, it sure made a big dent in my recovery.

In October of 2003, Peter invited me to his campsite in the woods near a bridge in Williamstown and I went. By then he had a tent and invited me in. Although it was a very small one-man tent, we managed. The geese were flying south; they gathered on the lake on the other side of the tracks before they left. An enormous honking sound began and before I knew it the geese started to fly in their formation.

Later when Peter and I were sitting outside, thirty chickadees surrounded us. When I was ten, my dad used to say, "Susan, listen to the birds talk, chickadees, d, d, d." When the chickadees sing I say, "Hi, Dad."

I told Peter this story and exclaimed, "My dad approves of our relationship. I've never seen so many chickadees and we are surrounded by them."

I thought that Dad was sending me a message, a big hug from him to me that he approved. My dad was a gentle man and compassionate in nature. As I would find out, Peter had the same qualities; I was a lucky woman to find such a man.

I wanted to learn all about Peter's way of life and I did. He became a real person. He used to call me *bella dona*, which means beautiful woman in Italian. He said *I love you* all the time, even when he was sober. He meant it. Peter said he and I would only have good memories. Unfortunately that didn't happen. Maybe it was silly of me to believe that I had met the love of my life.

There aren't even words to describe our sex life, it was that good. Although my whole life revolved around sex and I knew what good sex was, now there was a new ingredient: Love.

The love making was the best I've ever had, to this day. He said the same. We would make love nonstop for hours. We were in love with love and that made it special. I would tingle all over when we were done. He was a straight sex kind of guy. He was the first person I had sex with where I felt emotionally involved. It wasn't all about the sex. I loved that sex with him wasn't kinky. The majority of men I'd met were on the kinky side.

Sex with Peter felt like I was floating on a cloud. My climaxes were powerful. He used to say in a matter-of-fact way, "I don't have sex, I make love."

We would make love every day for up to three hours. He had the stamina of a young man. Even after ten years, he still wanted to make love three hours a day, every day. I was still up for it but not at his speed!

One day he was drunk as a skunk. He yelled into my window with a nasty loud voice, "I want sex!"

This didn't surprise me; I was used to that behavior. I could not reason with him in this state of mind, so I sent him on his way. There were times when he said, "I'm never coming back." But he always showed up the next day.

I brought Peter to see my therapist. This wasn't unusual because I wanted her to meet him, just like in every relationship I ever had. When she saw him, she almost fell out of her chair. I can't blame her. Both legs of his black jeans were covered with food and of course he smelled to high heaven.

My therapist's immediate reaction was surprise, but she tried not to show it. She must've been thinking, *Look what the cat dragged in. What in the world has Susan got herself into? How in the world could she have sex with that man?* I can't blame her; Peter was quite a sight to see.

I never recognized anything judgmental about her. Looking out for my best interest was her main goal. She advised me to just be friends but that didn't happen. Our relationship lasted ten years longer than any other I'd had; it didn't end until his death in 2012.

I can tell you one thing; it wasn't easy at first but the relationship was romantic. He had a lifestyle that I could never identify with, but the way he described it was magical. When we met in 2003 I was still psychotic, so I was easily pulled into his reality.

Peter believed that everything was alive and you shouldn't harm it. He was attuned with everything around him. For example, I had a vegetable garden. When I pulled up weeds he would get very angry with me.

We had disagreements and parted for a short while. I was angry because he was always leaving. But the day would come that he would stay.

Furious, I ran out to my garden and started pulling out all the weeds, saying in an angry voice, "This one's for you, Peter and that one's for you, Peter."

When he came back there wasn't a weed left in the garden. I said, "Don't start on me, this is my garden and I'll pull out the weeds if I want to."

In the worlds he lived in, trees could talk, so he wouldn't even step on an ant.

Peter wasn't a Buddhist; he was Roman Catholic. When I met him he had written in ink on the palms of his hands *Thanks God*. He would often say, "God help me." And when he opened a can of beer he would pour a little out and say, "Thanks, God."

I would reply in a nasty tone of voice, "Don't you mean 'Thanks, Susan'?"

The money he used to buy his beer was Social Security money that he received because I helped him get it.

Peter lived with me for five years. We were both more than a bit crazy at the time. I was still psychotic and he heard voices. He said there was a technology that wasn't commonly admitted to that put voices on your brain. He saw a therapist in the beginning of our relationship; they were unable to convince him that he had a mental illness, possibly schizophrenia. One of his coping mechanisms was no contact, no friction and this kept him out of trouble.

Peter admitted, "No one has taken me off the road for this long. I'm Odysseus and you're my siren."

One time Peter told me he could talk to ants. Even though I was psychotic, this seemed a little far-fetched. But I'd also had some way-out experiences; who could discount his? I would be angry if someone discounted mine, especially the paranormal ones.

One day we took a trip to Gloucester, to see Judith. Her family would not allow Peter into the house; he camped under a bridge for the weekend. She said to me, "Susan, he talks to ants! He's crazy! Get rid of him! He's a pig!"

I wasn't going to listen to her advice. Not me, I had other plans: to have the most wonderful, romantic life with my newfound friend.

At first, Peter slept on the front porch. He didn't like sleeping in houses. It was torture for him to be in a house and sleep in a bed. He loved me, however and with a psychotherapist's help he accomplished this, but with a lot of discomfort. He would sleep with me on a very tiny bed. The bed was smaller than twin size, but we managed it.

Every morning before I woke up he would have breakfast all prepared: sausage, eggs, fried beans and toast that had to be burnt. That's the way he liked his toast. After I tried it I liked it myself.

As I look back, no wonder I had high blood pressure! No exercising and painting all the time. The only part of my body that got exercised was the tips of my fingers when I used a paintbrush.

My three sons were living with me at the time. Peter would play the dictionary game with my son Andrew, betting a quarter on each word. Andrew had to give the definition of the word and spell it correctly. There were words I could hardly pronounce, but Peter knew the definitions and could spell them. He could define ten out of twelve words. It was amazing. I had nothing to do with this game—by the time I was finished, I would've lost my house. Neither spelling nor defining words were my forte.

When Peter was telling the truth, he said, "This ain't no bullshit, this is straight poop!" This was strange coming from someone that had such an awesome vocabulary.

When Peter was really sloshed and pouring down the vodka, he was more than just colorful. He was out-of-control, embarrassing and stuck on stupid. The next day he couldn't recollect his stupidity while intoxicated, so I gave up. But I had to start setting limits. There were rules now, no vodka or excessive beer drinking; if so he wasn't invited. At the end of his drinking he was breaking the rules; I would NOT talk or open the door for him in this condition.

At one point Peter's mom, Edna, lived in Onset, Cape Cod. Peter and I used to visit her for a week at a time. These visits were the best memories I have of Peter and me. We rode bicycles through the small town and took our dog Bella on long walks through the cranberry bogs.

These were mini vacations for us, away from the house and my adult children, who were all in the throes of their bipolar disorder. It was hell living in my own house. It became their home instead of mine. That's why these vacations were so important to us.

Edna was about 96 at the time and she had rules. One was that we could not sleep in the same bed because we were not married. We didn't sleep in the same room but we did manage to get together; Peter saw to that!

Peter set up a tent in the garage. He peed in a drain instead of going inside to the toilet. He was used to peeing outside; now there's a law against it. If he were caught in Massachusetts, he would become a level 1 sex offender.

The boys fought so their dad gave them boxing gloves. All the boys fought in the Vietnam War except Peter. He volunteered but the army said, "You're staying right here."

"Right here" was Alaska, where he was stationed and in charge of developing film. When the earthquake hit an eight on the Richter scale it was terrifying. Peter said after that he never wanted to be in a house again and he meant every word. Most of his life placed him on the road, his path for 26 years.

Peter was an artist. An artist on the Cape had taught him how to paint and make frames. When I was taking a class in painting, Peter showed me how to make frames and canvas from bed sheets. Canvas was very expensive, so sheets saved money. We painted the sheets white and when they dried we cut them to size and attached them to frames. We had a lot of fun doing this. As always, he was a joy to have around.

Peter wanted to make a six-foot painting. We put a white sheet on the floor, then painted our nude bodies and rolled onto the canvas. This was a lot of fun. He used to say, "If you're not having fun, you're in the wrong place."

Michael took our painting when we were through and burned it in the back yard, totally destroying it. Then he pulled a knife out and told Peter to leave. Peter did. I am one hundred percent sure Michael was no threat and was bluffing Peter. He didn't have any bad feelings for Peter; this was Michael's nature. He liked to push the limits. There was no more threatening behavior from him when Peter returned within a few weeks.

When I was 57, I received news that I had thyroid cancer. It was and still is papillary cancer. This type of cancer is the best out of four types of thyroid cancers. Anaplastic Thyroid Cancer is the worst kind you can have; it's very invasive.

When I heard the news that I had cancer I was stunned. I don't die, the people in the hospitals where I have worked for so many years die every day, not me. This was a shock; wasn't I immortal?

Peter brought me to Mass General hospital in Boston. He brought me to all my appointments. He was a great driver then and had no trouble driving in Boston's heavy traffic. Driving through downtown Boston was no easy task. But Peter had some ways of coping with the heavy traffic situation. He would make machine gun sounds and point his finger at the cars, blasting them out of his way.

Peter knew the city streets; he'd lived there as a kid and as an adult camped out there for months. He set his campsite in back of a package store, which was a short distance to buy his Genesee beer and an occasional bottle of vodka, then he'd visit his friends at the car wash.

Fortunately, the cancer was found early enough that I recovered. Joyce, a nurse and Peter's sister-in-law, hooked me up with a great surgeon who took out the rest of my thyroid. Five years and counting, all the ultrasound and blood work are normal. My endocrinologist at Mass. General Hospital in Boston is wonderful.

I had radio iodine therapy. I drank radio iodine and it killed all thyroid cells that might have still been present. I had to be in the lead room, which was on the 21st floor. It had a couch, a chair and the most spectacular view, especially at night when all the buildings' lights were on. I asked my doctor, "What did I do to get this view?"

Yet I felt like Typhoid Mary. If someone got close enough it's possible that the iodine I drank could close down their airways. I could never be near children. There were certain precautions I had to take. I had to flush the toilet three times when I urinated because iodine could be excreted through my urine. My tooth brush couldn't be thrown away for three months. And Peter couldn't sleep with me or have sex for three days after the Iodine therapy.

I was talking to an acquaintance of mine and said with hilarity, "You have nothing to worry about as long as I don't pee on you." I went on to explain this is how the iodine is excreted. He gave me a dirty look.. When he drank vodka I became his captive; in this state of mind it was very embarrassing to be out in public with him. He would yell, "Look me in the eye!" and every other word was fucking this and fucking that.

As time went on his drinking put pressure on our relationship and I made a decision to let him go. I still loved Peter, but I couldn't live with him because of his predicament with the bottle. Genesee was his mistress and in the end his mistress killed him. It was time to part. I put the love of my life on a train to Texas. This was a very sad day for me, an emotional ripping at my heart.

Peter told me, "You're losing a drunk, but not a friend."

We would still be together if it weren't for Peter's heavy alcohol consumption. He defended himself, saying with conviction, "My lungs hurt and alcohol is my medication." He said I was a drug addict because I took medication and he used that to excuse his drinking. However, I have never taken an illegal drug in my life; the only drugs I took were for Manic Depression.

Peter used to call me a civilian and himself, a mountain man. As time passed, he became a civilian, too.

He always carried a cell phone and kept in touch with his children and grandchildren in Texas. Suddenly he couldn't live without it. At approximately 4:00AM, he would charge his cell phone in the electrical socket on my back porch. When one of his grandchildren first texted him on his cell phone, he had no idea how to text back. He found it quite amusing and marveled, "What will they think of next?"

This was the guy whose only connection to the outside world used to be a radio powered with old batteries he'd found along the roadside.

Most people would say Peter had a lost life but this wasn't true. Peter enjoyed his way of life and did whatever he chose; this might sound selfish, but it kept him out of trouble.

I'm not a psychiatrist but Peter used to hear voices, some female, since the age of ten. I had a sneaking suspicion he drank because he had a mental illness.

My therapist said, "If he's off the road for two years he won't be able to go back."

She was right. He spent six months out of the year with his son William. When he got too hot in Texas he came to visit me. While he was away he wrote me letters and most of the time, ended the letter: *I miss you like a son of a bitch.*

How romantic. But that was his way of communicating.

I only let him sleep in my house on some occasions. However, we continued to have a strong emotional connection. We could've had a life together, but his mistress Genesee took him away from me. He was no longer the man I loved. It was a sad state of affairs that he was drunk more than he was sober!

Sometimes I wonder if I was wrong to help him get Disability. He spent all his money on beer and vodka. When he drank vodka he was out-of-control and I was unable to reason with him. When he was drunk he wanted everyone to listen to him. I could've put a knife to his chest and tell him to shut up, but he would've kept talking. I used to feel guilty, but after a while I didn't. He made his choice and it wasn't me.

Sometimes Peter became jealous and accused me of things I never did. I was faithful, but he didn't believe me.

The straw that broke the camel's back was when he slept with his ex-wife while in El Paso. Things were not the same after that. I trusted him and he betrayed me.

Trust was always a major issue with me. I couldn't trust him anymore and the relationship went down the toilet. Yes, I gave it a flush. My emotional ties were beginning to break and he no longer constantly shared a space in my head all the time. But that didn't mean I didn't love him.

Years passed and I saw the foolishness of it all. How could I have believed someone who talked to ants, plants and animals and believed in interspecies communication? Yet I was. I was open-minded, but talking to ants?

After Peter, I had no room for anyone else. Peter was my love. He was instrumental in my healing process. I walked down a holistic avenue that put stability into the mix, finally correcting the problem.

At one time I explained to my therapist that in a relationship I give eighty percent and save the other twenty so I don't hurt as much once it ends. She disagreed with me. "It won't work. You'll be like a dog that goes to a corner to lick your wounds."

I stopped because she was right. I couldn't break up with anyone. I always had to make them mad at me so they would leave.

The therapist would ask, "What is going to happen if you tell them to leave? Is the sky going to fall? Are they going to hit you?"

I couldn't get through this until Peter taught me to say, "Enough" and "NO." In the spring of 2012, Peter returned. We still saw each other; that didn't change. The love and respect remained. But I had to put limits on his visits. He didn't eat much and drank every day. Sober, he was welcome and I stuck to this decision.

We still had good times together. We looked for stones together; he would wade knee-deep into a stream to get a rock I liked. We made a stone wall around my flower garden, then we placed each rock and pebble in just the right place.

The last thing I remember was us smelling the roses in the garden. He said, "Wow, I can smell it!" Because of his smoking he was unable to smell things very well, so this surprised him.

We still had a sexual relationship. That never changed; the intimacy was too overwhelming to ignore. It was as if we were spiritual twins.

In June of 2012, Peter, the love of my life, knocked at my door. That was the first time I didn't let him in; he was just too intoxicated. When he was in that state of mind he held me hostage and commanded, "Look me in the eye."

He would repeat, over and over, "Susan, I want to ask you just one question."

This time I was really angry that he showed up in this condition. I refused to answer him, so he stayed on my back deck until dark. Eugene made him his favorite snack, burnt toast and handed it to him through the window. The last thing I saw was his little black cap as I peered out the second floor window.

There were many times when Peter came to see me severely intoxicated. It was incredible how much this man could drink and still stand up, then carry on a conversation.

However, the drink started to affect his mobilization. When Eugene and Peter went to the coffeehouse in Williamstown, Eugene had to be at his side when he walked. Peter was staggering for the first time and almost fell into the street. The worst thing that could happen to Peter was to break his hip and end up in a hospital or nursing home.

Peter spent the spring, winter and fall near Moody Bridge on Cole Avenue in Williamstown, Massachusetts. His camp was about 600 yards from the bridge, near the railroad tracks.

One afternoon in June, a North Adams police officer came up my driveway. He asked, "Are you Susan Rose?"

I said I was. He handed me a piece of paper with the phone number of the Massachusetts State Police and said I was to speak with a sergeant handling an investigation. I said, stunned, "Can you repeat that again?" I thought one of my children was in some kind of trouble.

I was very apprehensive when I took the phone in my hand and dialed the number. The voice on the other end of the phone asked, "Are you Susan Rose? Do you know Peter Mitchell?"

I responded in a happy voice, "Yes, I know him."

The sergeant asked, "How are you related to him?"

I said, "He's been my friend for ten years." Of course he was more than a friend, but I didn't say that to the sergeant.

The sergeant said, in a mellow tone of voice, six horrifying words. "He was killed by a train."

He couldn't say anything else. I became highly hysterical, crying and saying to Eugene, "Peter has been killed by a train." As I settled down the sergeant spoke again; I interrupted him. "Is his body mangled?"

The officer replied, "He was struck in the head and has no face."

Later I found out that the officer was being kind. Peter's body was in pieces and it took weeks to identify him; the only way he could be identified was his fingerprints. He was only 67 when he was struck and killed by the train on Saturday, June 9, 2012 near Moody Bridge, at approximately two o'clock in the morning. He lost the battle with the bottle. It's very possible he staggered and fell on the railroad tracks, though he was a man who always took precautions so accidents like these would never happen.

It was a tearful moment when his four children from Texas went to the site where he was killed to pick up his belongings: a bike, two sleeping bags, two scarves and two hats. He didn't have many belongings. Peter left behind his spirit; no one could take that away from us. His eldest son said in a tearful voice, "I came all the way from Texas to see his blue eyes."

But that was impossible; there was nothing left to be seen.

Now I think back to the night of his death; all he'd wanted was to ask me one question. I know what he would ask and as always, my answer would've been, "Yes, I love you."

As the old saying goes, you don't know what you have until you lose it. However, all along I knew that with Peter I had the first intimate relationship in my life with someone I loved, someone who taught me to say "NO."

From the North Adams Transcript:

A tragic senseless death

My friend and the love of my life was hit by a train near Moody Bridge in Williamstown Massachusetts and lost his life. He was camped out in the woods near the tracks. He wasn't a homeless man he preferred living outdoors. He used to say the sky is my wallpaper. He lived this eccentric life for 26 years until he met me 10 years ago. This was a beginning of a wonderful friendship with a gentle, kind, compassionate human being.

Life won't be the same without him; everyone he met he would say in a safe warm way, "Give me a hug." It was hard for him to make a transition from the road into the confines of a house but he did this because he loved me. He used to call me Bella Dona; in Italian this meant beautiful woman. We spent many hours making frames and canvas and also painting colorful abstracts.

In 2003 he had his paintings displayed at Papyri bookstore when it was on Main Street in North Adams Massachusetts. He sold one of his paintings called "The Huggers" for $75. There was also a front-page article in the North Adams transcript paper; on his way of life and our friendship.

At first he would sleep on my front porch and set up a tent in my backyard; then gradually slept on the floor in my home. Sleeping indoors was painful for him. He used to call me a civilian because I lived in a house and owned many things. But after two years he became accustomed to these creature comforts; eight years later he couldn't live without a cell phone. I helped him get disability and Mass health so he didn't have to pick up cans for a living. Unfortunately he had a dilemma with the bottle and the new income gave him the ability to buy more alcohol. He said, "Susan, this will become a wedge between us." And he was right.

This extra money also helped him to visit with his children in Texas; and lived with his eldest son and took the role of grandpa. Peter's mother is 105 and over the years I was fortunate to meet her. We had many wonderful conversations; she lived on a farm and used to ride the cows. She also had 10 children, nine boys and a girl. She is still very lucid and walks with a cane. The tragedy of a mother living so long is heart breaking; especially when you have to bury so many of your children. She still has about five other children who are still alive.

The people that came into contact with Peter had only good things to say about him. He was charismatic; it was his nature. Many people in the Berkshires will miss Peter's warm smile.

Two days before the accident he said in an angry voice, "I am tired of being a yo-yo! I am never coming back!"

Two days after Peter's death I was awakened by a dream. I was gently pulled out of bed, still in a dream state. I wrote something down. I have done this before, writing down just a few words after waking and in the morning it was a bunch of scribbles. I thought this would be the same. But that afternoon, I saw in beautiful script, with every word capitalized and words underlined to emphasize importance, in the way Peter wrote: <u>SLEEPING</u> FOR EVER <u>WAKE</u> UP. How could it be this legible after being written in the dark, down to the underlining?

Peter always wrote in capital letters. He wrote this poem about himself:

<u>BY PETER</u>

WHEN I WAS A YOUNG LAD

TIME WAS WARM AND GOLD

I AM ETERNAL YOUTH I SAID

I'M NEVER GROWING OLD

ONE DAY I MET A VAGABOND

WHOSE WRINKLES SPOKE OF AGES

TIME IS ALL YOU HAVE HE SAID

DON'T SPEND IT EARNING WAGES

AS HE WINKED HIS WIZENED EYE

AND RUBBED HIS BEARDED CHIN

I COULDN'T HELP BUT FEEL

THAT HE AND I WERE KIN

HIS HEAD WAS CROWNED WITH CURLS

HE HAD DUSTY SANDAL FEET

LOVE LIFE MY CHILD HE SMILED

AS HE STARTED DOWN THE STREET

DON'T GO PLEASE STAY I YELLED

BUT HE DIDN'T HEAR MY CALL

I SADLY WATCHED HIS FIGURE
AS IT KEPT GROWING SMALL
WE'LL MEET AGAIN I VOWED
WE'LL SOON SPEAK FACE TO FACE
THEN I HIT THE ROAD
TO GIVE THAT BUM A CHASE
BUT THROUGH THE MANY DISTANT YEARS
THE TRUTH I FINALLY SEE
THAT VAGABOND I MET THAT DAY
WAS JUST AN OLDER ME

Peter never heard the horn that day. He was too far from the railroad crossing and it was pitch black.

I hear the train Wessel go by frequently. When the whistle blows I yell, "Peter get off the tracks!"

As I write this story and read his letters, I feel that ache in my abdomen. It's a sign of depression and sometimes I have to stop. It's impossible to write these recollections after 6:00 PM; I can't fall asleep.

Peter once said, "I want to die drunk on the mountain."

He did die drunk and got his other wish; he was looking forward to the biggest adventure… "When my spirit leaves my body, it will go poosh…!"

Peter said many times, "Susan, wear a callous around your heart; you never know when I'll kick the bucket."

He wanted to spare me the pain if he should die before me, but his suggestion of the callous around my heart didn't work. It's been over a year now since his death and I still cry like an infant missing its mother's warmth and tender touch.

I finally understood Peter's unusual perspective on life. It was simple; nothing was a problem, everything was an adventure. He'd hold up an object and say, "Look at each end facing us, we both see different things. Life is just an adventure ma'am. If we look at it this way we both win."

Love is a strange thing. It's the unconditional love that baffles me, when we find minutes when we are truly happy. We no longer think of self. How great it is to give, expecting nothing in return. There are too many people who don't think this way. It sure would make a happier existence. But nowadays no one wants to make a commitment in relationships and what does that tell you? I, I and I are today's lifestyle.

When Peter was offered a job he told me, "I'd love to work with him but my hourglass is running out of time. If I can see you every now and then I'm a wealthy man."

When we were about to have an adventure, he would say, "Roll, the dice, baby doll."

I'm looking forward to my greatest adventure arriving, when my spirit leaves my body and joins his on the adventure of our lives and we love until the end of time.

Reality is trying to understand the unacceptable. Life changes without the answers. Today I ask for help because I can't do it alone. My psychotic break brought me to my knees. I stand up straight but that doesn't mean I can't fall. This disease is insidious and sneaks up on me, slaps me in the face then back to my knees. But I will stand again. This is why I am hyper-vigilant, always alert, no matter how balanced I may be. Madness still dwells within me. It may lie dormant, but at any time it can erupt like an inferno. The burning lava will surround my brain and fuel madness. There will be no regulator and control will no longer be in my grasp. Disaster and chaos will ensue. Nobody would want to trudge up that road back to sanity; only few make it back. It's spiritual warfare, malevolence. I was fortunate; a force so powerful and loving was on my side through it all. Yes, I met my creator. We walked together through the wilderness and saw me to the other side.

Putting life's difficulties and traumas on a few pages is nearly impossible; mine are too numerous for the pages to contain. Some memories will never leave me, some will never to be told, recalled only by me and I let them go. Passageways in my mind have sealed, hiding memories not ready to be revealed until prompted. Writing about my life has brought the humiliation back. New memories are overwhelming as a result. But I must tell me story so others can see there is hope… and we can triumph.

EPILOGUE

It's 2012 and I haven't been hospitalized in four years, cutting medications in half. I was too sedated with medication that I no longer require; my life stressors are reduced and high levels of medication no longer necessary. I have clarity now. The last few years I have reclaimed my voice and I am using it. I am truly blessed!

Andrew, Michael and Jack affectionately refer to me as Mental Mom.
My children still struggle with financial issues. It's hard to live on disability payments of $650 a month. Jack lives with me and his cat named Ma Cluster, Ester Ma Cluster and Big-z. The cats have helped all of us.

Eugene has lived with me since he was released from prison seven years ago. Andrew lives alone and graduated with a BS in psychology three years ago. Michael lives with his dad today. Their aggressive behavior disappeared years ago and they are a pleasure now; they take their medication and Jack sees a therapist regularly. It's been a year since Peter, the love of my life, was hit by the train.

I still miss Peter. He was special. I have dated a few men and ended the relationships within a few months. I guess I have been spoiled.

Peter, Love; I wish you were still here. It's so hum drum without you. You had the magic touch, the one that opened my heart. Rest in peace, my love. God speed.

Further Reading

Kay Redfield Jamison is my savior and hero. She wrote “Touched with Fire,” “Darkness Falls Fast” and “Nothing Was the Same.” She also wrote the most comprehensive book available on Bipolar Disorder in her autobiography “An Unquiet Mind.” Just the title captivated me. I was not an avid reader; my mind was not still. It was always on the run. Yet I read her autobiography in approximately one night. Her writing style was very poetic. It had such a profound effect on my son Michael that he took the book with him to school every day and would not let go of it even when his teacher punished him.

When I took Lithium my mind stopped. No more noise! This was foreign to me. It was a pleasure to be able to read; this was the first time my mind wasn’t going faster than the paragraphs. I was able to concentrate. I related to the things Jamison wrote about. She was a courageous person to tell her story and risk her job as a psychiatrist. The risk that I take is multiplied because I tell all, not keeping my story edited of any events.

In April of 2008 Bonnie Obremski from the North Adams transcript asked Kay Redfield Jamison for an interview. She titled her article Mental Health: Doctor Speaks at Williams; Rose: Artist pleased with attention given to disorder. I was able to get an interview before anyone else because I got a tip from my therapist that Dr. Jamison was coming to speak at Williams College. Her lecture was entitled “Personal and Professional Perspective on Mental Illness.” It was part of a three day program “Mental Health Matters: Reducing Stress, Distress and Stigma at Williams.”

After I attended the lecture I asked someone to take a photograph of Kay Redfield Jamison and me. This was the most emotional moment of my life. She and I spoke the same language of what it's like to live with Bipolar Disorder. I hope she reads Madness Broke the Rose. I have no degrees after my name; just a simple tale of living with a foe.

Video of interest: "The Lobotomies"

Dr. Freeman was called the moral monster. He used an ice pick and hammer without sterile techniques. He used shock treatment to render the patient unconscious for four minutes. It only took three minutes to perform the procedure. It scares me that I could have been his victim at an early age if my mother complained about my behavior.

Dr. Walter Freeman was performing frontal lobotomies without anesthesia. He was using electroconvulsive therapy without consent as early as 1946. He created a replacement technique that was quicker and more cost effective, without an operating room or anesthetic. Lobotomies done in an operating room were too costly, as were the sterile instruments, a nurse and an anesthesiologist.

Dr. Freeman perfected another method. His instruments of choice consisted of an ice pick and a hammer, with no sterile techniques and no operating room. The procedure itself only took three to four minutes and when the patient awoke, they didn't know what happened. Some doctors were unable to watch. Others vomited and had to leave the room. A child could have the skill needed to perform this technique. Oh, what a horrible thought! But all you needed was an ice pick and hammer.
The elongated ice pick was pressed upward, sandwiched between the eye ball and eyelid, reaching into the eye socket. Dr. Freeman would use the hammer to hit the ice pick then puncture the bony surface and reach into the frontal lobes. As he broke through the cranium into the frontal lobes, he would swing the ice pick back and forth by the handle and destroy the frontal lobes, with devastating effects. This method was only to be used as the last resort; yet in one asylum he said, "Bring me all your psychotic patients."

There were seventy-five and he did them all in one day, without consent. The patients were mentally ill and had no voices. There was no one to stop him and no one asked questions.

This barbaric act destroyed the patients' intellect. Some became childlike and were unable to go home. Most were not as lucky.

Even though other doctors knew and opposed, Dr. Freeman's reign continued. Back then doctors only talked between themselves, never to the media. This is probably why it went on so long.

I learned about this from the PBS home video called "The Lobotomies." I didn't read the back of the video, where a doctor was pointing to an x-ray of the skull. I thought it was a medical procedure and borrowed the video from the library. When I put it in my DVD player I was shocked. That the visual impact and the personal content were nauseating was an understatement.
Freeman's methods didn't just affect the mentally ill. He performed them on soldiers

that had battle fatigue and children as young as four years old. He was a very ambitious doctor but in the end he was called a moral monster!

Fortunately patients are now treated more humanely. When the drug Thorazine, a heavily sedating antipsychotic medication, was introduced, it was called the chemical lobotomy. This replaced Dr. Freedman's reign of horror. Even after they removed him and took his license away, he still practiced in California. One of his patients hemorrhaged and died. Then he went on a quest to find his old patients and see how they were getting along. This was the last of his legacy.